Average Joe

The Coach Joe Kennedy Story

AVERAGE JOE

ONE MAN'S FAITH
AND THE FIGHT TO
CHANGE A NATION

Joe Kennedy

SALEM
BOOKS
an imprint of Regnery Publishing
Washington, D.C.

Salem Books™ is a trademark of Salem Communications Holding Corporation. Regnery® and its colophon are registered trademarks of Salem Communications Holding Corporation.
Cataloging-in-Publication data on file with the Library of Congress.

ISBN: 978-1-68451-509-7
eISBN: 978-1-68451-510-3

Published in the United States by
Salem Books
An Imprint of Regnery Publishing
A Division of Salem Media Group
Washington, D.C.
www.SalemBooks.com

Manufactured in the United States of America

10 9 8 7 6 5 4 3 2 1

Books are available in quantity for promotional or premium use. For information on discounts and terms, please visit our website: www.SalemBooks.com

I want to dedicate this book to Denise, my first and five-ever love; to our kids, Jacob, Emily, Zachary and Ethan; to my awesome father-in-law, Ron; to Ty and the Reed family for being my family when nobody else wanted me; to the Fords and Farmers for taking me in; to my Buddhist Jedi-Master, Pappy; and to everyone at the youth ranch where I spent time as a kid. You guys saved my life in more ways than one, and for that I am forever grateful.

I also must reluctantly dedicate this book to all my "ex-wives" at First Liberty, especially my favorite "wife," Jeremy. Without you all, there would be no case and no book. God certainly has a sense of humor. Also to Jeff, A. J., Devon and all the attorneys at Dunder-Mifflin Law Group . . . or whatever it's really called.

To my Bremerton football players from 2008–2015. I love you guys.

Lastly to JG and MLG, the wild men LT and ST, and a shout-out to my two main ghosts, Jenn and Steph. Maybe now you'll return my texts, yeah?

CONTENTS

CONTENTS

FOREWORD

God regularly uses "average" guys and gals to do extraordinary things. That's what happened with Coach Joe Kennedy.

First Liberty Institute's involvement with Joe started when I heard our attorneys were leaving on an emergency trip to Bremerton, Washington, because a high school football coach was in trouble. The coach thought he might be fired because he had made a pledge to God to pray after every game when people are slapping each other on the back on the field, making dinner reservations on their phone, and saying hello to old friends. For seven years, Coach Kennedy faithfully fulfilled that promise to God, thanking Him for the privilege of coaching the young men on his team. But now the school was telling him that if he did it again, he would be fired. As a former career Marine, Coach Kennedy rightfully believed that the freedoms he had fought to defend were being stripped away from him.

Because we have lots of former military on staff at First Liberty and we have specialized our legal practice in defense of constitutional freedom, our attorneys love to be part of cases like Coach's. Though our team was excited about Coach's case, as the founder and president of First Liberty, I saw the risks. Washington is part of the Ninth U.S. Circuit Court of Appeals—not only the largest and most powerful federal appellate court in the country, but also the most liberal. Its judges had earned a reputation of curtailing religious liberties and already had a long record of making bad decisions on the subject. The odds of Coach's case making it past them to the U.S. Supreme Court were astronomically against us.

Just to give you an idea, in 2022, eight thousand petitioners appealed to the Supreme Court, and only sixty-six of their cases were actually heard. If Coach's case didn't make it to that level, it might create even stricter limitations on religious liberties . . . but if it did make it, we had the chance to clean up legislation on this facet of the Constitution for the whole country. That was a chance we couldn't pass up.

My first meeting with Joe took place in 2015 on the set of *The O'Reilly Factor*—the number one-rated cable show at the time. Joe had been working with other attorneys on our team, but this was the first time I was meeting him face-to-face. As we sat in the green room, I learned that Joe is a quirky, goofy guy who loves to joke and mess around. To this day, he won't let me live down the fact that O'Reilly called me "Kerry" instead of Kelly on the air. Ever since that first meeting, I have been "Kerry" to Joe.

But what really struck me as I have gotten to know him better over the years is that there is no pretense with Joe. There's no angle, no self-righteous message he's trying to force onto other people. He'll be the first to tell you that he's no theologian—he'd probably joke that he doesn't even know what that word means. His faith is his own, deep and heartfelt, yet at the same time childlike and full of wonder. It's the faith of a guy with a rough childhood, abandoned by his parents and shuffled through foster homes and group homes; a guy who joined the Marines because he needed discipline to grow up and make something of a life that was heading in the wrong direction. By all accounts, he was the least likely candidate to be thrust into the spotlight of a religious liberties case, but he was just the guy God wanted: a guy who would fight and persevere when things were hard, when tensions flared, and when it almost cost him everything. And, in the end, God rewarded his faith and his obedience to the call.

Coach Kennedy's case is one of the biggest First Amendment cases in U.S. history. If you've followed any of his story in the news, you might only know that, after seven years of litigation, he won his case. The Supreme Court recognized that Coach's prayers on the field were not unconstitutional. Now he not only gets to coach again, but he can continue to take a knee after the game in prayer. The school is enjoined by law from interfering with that from now on.

However, what most people don't know is that the Court's final decision has much greater ramifications nationwide. Yes, Coach Joe's case was the first in our nation's history in which the First Amendment rights and religious freedoms of coaches and teachers were clarified and protected—but the victory is bigger than that. His is the most significant victory for religious freedom in over fifty years.

In that decision, the Supreme Court overruled another major case, *Lemon v. Kurtzman*, which has been cited more than seven thousand times in the last fifty years and created hostility toward religious expression across America. Many Americans are aware of growing attacks to remove Nativity scenes and menorahs from public venues each December, or Ten Commandments monuments nationwide. These attacks and hostilities were all based on the *Lemon* case, which courts applied through what was appropriately called the "Lemon" test.

Thanks to Coach Kennedy, *Lemon* is now dead. Five of the Supreme Court justices agreed that it was not only an outdated method of judging religious expression, but now all seven thousand citations over the past fifty years have to be reconsidered. Where crosses were once torn down, they can now go back up. Where Ten Commandments displays were put into storage, they can now come back out. Where prayers were banned through the threat of job termination, workers can now pray again.

This all happened because of one average Joe with a heart for God and his country who knew how to fight and to persevere, and knew the importance of the freedoms he fought for. It was in his DNA, just as it is in all of ours as Americans. We don't back down from a fight when it is over our freedoms and the freedoms of others.

Even though Coach Joe's case has made history for resetting a lot of the tests and laws formerly used to determine freedom of expression in religious liberty cases, we still have a long way to go. First Liberty continues to defend religious liberties cases on behalf of Americans of all walks of faith, not just the Judeo-Christian faith. Constitutional freedoms apply to all, and all people must continue to stand, fight, and sacrifice if we are to protect this incredible country that has been built on freedoms envied the world over. Joe's story shows that Americans still get their day in court—and can win if they're willing to fight for what they believe in.

—Kelly Shackelford
President/CEO
First Liberty Institute

INTRODUCTION

In the 2021–22 session, approximately six thousand cases were appealed to the U.S. Supreme Court. Of those, only sixty-eight were accepted.[1] Mine was one of them—and even more extraordinarily, it would be the second time it had come before the Court.

I'd been fighting for my religious freedom since 2015. When my attorneys called in January 2019 to inform me that the Supreme Court had denied the writ to hear our case, I thought that fight had come to an end. Instead, the justices did an unheard-of thing by attaching a statement telling us what we needed to do in order to get them to hear the case later. In all the years my legal team had been practicing law (which is an absurdly long time if you add it all up—more than a century, collectively), they had never seen this happen. I should have played the lottery that day, with my luck! Usually, the Court just denies your case without any explanation, and that's that. It's over.

---

1 Ballotpedia, "Supreme Court Cases, October Term 2021–2022," https://ballot-pedia.org/Supreme_Court_cases,_October_term_2021-2022.

In my case, they not only gave us a lifeline but a roadmap of what we needed to do for *next time.*

My next time came in May 2022. I climbed the thirty-six steps to the Supreme Court building proudly wearing my blue Bremerton High School football polo shirt with my wife—the love of my life, Denise—by my side. Eight football seasons in the making, we were finally about to have our day in court.

I gave Denise a kiss and posed for the dozens of photographers that had accumulated at a socially acceptable distance. As my attorney went into the historic courthouse, I was ushered across the street to a conference room where I would listen to my own trial on C-SPAN. That's right: After eight football seasons spent in litigation and two trips to the Supreme Court, I was not allowed to attend my own hearing due to COVID-19 restrictions. Instead, I listened from a block away as my fate was decided by people who did not really know me despite all the briefs that had been prepared and evidence collected.

As I clutched Denise's hand and did my best to decipher the endless stream of legalese being exchanged between the attorneys and justices, I couldn't help but reflect on the crazy journey that had landed me here.

I was the kid nobody wanted. I had been given up for adoption at birth, was always getting into fights, was expelled from six different schools, and was sent to several foster homes and group homes before being sent away to a state-run boys' home. I barely graduated high school with a 0.4 GPA before joining the military at seventeen. I fought in Kuwait and have been married three times. I proposed to Denise when I first laid eyes on her at the age of nine. It was one of those Hollywood rom-com moments in which time slowed down as she looked up at me with her big brown eyes as I got off my BMX bike. She was the most beautiful girl I had ever seen, and I knew she was and would always be the first and only love of my life. It would take thirty-something years for us to finally end up together—and the case that had brought me here had almost cost me that.

When people ask why I almost gave up the love of my life to fight for prayer in schools, it's because Denise had been my own answer to prayer. I had cried out to God to bring us together. When she had a mini-stroke, I retired from my twenty-year career in the Marines the next day so I could be there for her. When the post-stroke depression she struggled with was damaging our relationship, I stood at the altar of our church and solemnly promised God that I would obey Him no matter what if He would just save our marriage. I didn't think He'd take that promise so literally. It's hilarious that God picked me, of all people, to become the face of prayer in school, but when I felt that my right to religious expression was being taken away and nobody else would stand up for it, I did what I had trained my whole life to do: I fought.

I did not anticipate that my long-suffering wife, who had been a devout Christian her entire life while I went through "phases" of dedicating myself to God, would misunderstand that fight. She didn't understand why I was so adamant about fighting the school district, yet it was impossible for me, at that time, to explain that it was because of the bargain I had made with God for our marriage. I had finally gone "all in" for God and now it felt like He was using me as a modern-day Job from the Bible. I had lost the coaching job that was my life—my calling!—because I took a knee in prayer on the fifty-yard line after every football game. In doing this, I had put Denise between a rock and a hard place. In addition to standing behind me as her husband, she also happened to be the head of the Bremerton (Washington) School District human resources department—the very entity that had fired me for praying. She was put in the horrible position of being asked to leave school board meetings regarding my case because the school district saw she had a conflict of interest—and I couldn't discuss my case with her, either, because my lawyers saw it the same way. She received death threats and emails saying she should burn in Hell because of what I'd done. As a result, she became withdrawn and severely depressed. Meanwhile, I lived with the constant pain of being away from the kids on my team, losing my position and purpose as a coach, and now losing my wife.

The marriage I had surrendered to God was now on the rocks. I was about to leave Denise to spare her further pain. She had faced enough pain, and I could not put her through any more of it. After months of silence, merely coexisting as roommates in the same household, things finally came to a head. After failing to satisfy her question of "Why?" yet again, I grabbed my keys with every intention of giving her space to heal from me. I hadn't packed a bag or made any plans; I was just going to get in my truck and drive.

As I left her in tears on the bed, I got a text. I'll never forget how annoyed I was that someone had texted me in that exact moment, when my whole world seemed to be falling apart. When I looked at my phone to see who had texted me, a video message began to play. Instantly, my knees went out from under me as I fell down our steps, sobbing. I even broke the banister as I collapsed to the wooden floor below. All I could do was sit there, tears streaming down my face. I couldn't stand back up. I couldn't speak. I was a completely broken man.

Denise came running when she heard me fall. I think she thought I had had a heart attack. She was asking if she should call 911. I literally couldn't speak through the sobs. All I could do was push play on the video and hand her my phone.

We both watched the video in absolute awe and amazement; its message changed everything instantly. It said everything I had been trying and failing to explain to Denise for months. She suddenly understood why this case was so important to me, and almost immediately, our relationship was transformed. It was as if God was testing me to see if I would really keep my promise to Him—and, in seeing that I would by putting Him above the love of my life in that moment, He suddenly restored our marriage yet again.

Those prayers I prayed on the fifty-yard line after the Bremerton High School football games were never for attention, and certainly never to proselytize[2] impressionable minors. Ask anyone who knows me; they'll tell you that I'm not the most religious guy. I believe in freedom of religious expression for people of all faiths, not just my own. As a twenty-year Marine Corps veteran who fought in the First Gulf War, I simply took issue with my constitutional rights being assaulted—the rights I had risked my life to support and defend against all enemies, foreign and domestic, when I took my Oath of Enlistment. I didn't understand why the same rights guaranteed to everyone else in this country were suddenly being taken away from me. Yet, if you had told me—or anyone else who knew me as a young man—that I'd become the poster guy for religious freedom in America, the infamous "Praying Coach," I'd have laughed.

Though I was raised in church, I didn't meet God until I was fourteen, when I thought my parents moved away without telling me, leaving me behind. In a blind rage, I broke into their old house and destroyed everything in sight. I was a screaming, sobbing, exhausted mess in the middle of the living room, cursing at God and asking Him to show Himself. After being carried off by the sheriff to a state-run group home, my adopted parents eventually sent me to a paramilitary-style boy's home upstate in the mountains. Despite the rage that consumed me, God began showing Himself to me through what I can describe as nothing other than a series of divinely inspired "coincidences."

I never learned to formally pray. My prayers have always been short, simple, and conversational, as if I'm just talking to God. I don't

---

2 I had no idea what this word meant until my lawyers explained it to me.

quote a lot of Scripture. To be perfectly honest, I don't know a lot of Scripture! As a kid, I hated reading, so to this day I don't even really read the Bible. I'm a simple guy with a simple philosophy when it comes to religion: I try to love God and love others to the best of my ability, and I still fail at that all the time.

Yet for some reason, as I was watching the movie *Facing the Giants* one Friday night in 2008, I felt what I can only describe as His hand reaching through my TV screen and grabbing hold of my heart. In that instant, I knew that I, like the coach in the movie, was being called to give thanks to God after every game, win or lose. I had no idea that the promise I made to Him on my knees late that night in front of my living room TV screen would have national and historical ramifications.

I didn't know that this unwanted, troublesome kid would one day be invited to the Oval Office to meet the president of the United States . . .

. . . that this jarhead who loved to fight would be called to fight for something with such purpose . . .

. . . that this guy who barely graduated high school would be quoted in legal textbooks for the next hundred years. . .

. . . or that this average Joe's life would be used by God in extraordinary and unfathomable ways.

If you think my story is too unbelievable to be true, just think how I feel—and I lived it! This is my chance to tell my story and show how God continues to use the most unlikely people, like me, to change the world.

CHAPTER 1

DO NOT REHIRE

I never wanted to coach high school football. I had never played high school football. I didn't even really watch football. In high school, I was on the wrestling team because I was four-foot-eleven until my junior year. Playing football was just not in my cards. Don't get me wrong, it's not that I didn't like football—I like watching it as much as anyone with ADD and ADHD can sit still long enough to watch anything—but it was not something I ever gave much thought to, especially as a potential job.

In 2006, I had just gotten out of the Marine Corps after twenty years of service and started a new job at the Puget Sound Naval Shipyard. I was struggling to readjust to working with clueless civilians, and discovered running was a good personal outlet for my frustrations. I trained for a lot of marathons and half marathons and was on one of my long training runs when, out of the blue one morning, a smiling stranger honked his car horn at me and pulled alongside to ask me if I wanted to come coach high school football for him.

I didn't know this man from Adam, but that day I just happened to be wearing a Bremerton High School T-shirt that my wife, Denise, had bought me. The man introduced himself as George Duarte, the athletic director at Bremerton High, and began trying to carry on a conversation with me as I was jogging along. I asked him to meet me at a sports bar a few miles up the road where I would finish my route. I hoped he'd just go about his day, but when I got to the sports bar, there he was, waiting for me.

"You went to Bremerton?" he asked.

"Yeah," I replied. "I went there my senior year and graduated in '88."

"You ever play football?"

"No, but I was on the wrestling team at Naches High."

A look of recognition crossed Smiling George Duarte's face as he noticed I was wearing wrestling shoes rather than traditional running shoes. He asked, "So what have you been doing with yourself?"

"I just got out of the Marines."

"Oh yeah?" He sat up with interest. "How long were you in?"

"Twenty years."

"And you're still out there running like that?"

I laughed, not really sure why he was asking or why I owed an explanation.

"I was serious, you know," he continued, "about you coming to coach for Bremerton. Have you ever thought about coaching football?"

"I don't know anything about football."

"We need someone with leadership skills. We already have a brilliant crew of guys doing the X's and O's, but I need some people who can train these young men to be better young men. They need help with the intangible things."

Until that point, I had been feigning interest and mostly thinking Duarte was maybe a little bit crazy for offering a job to a total stranger with no experience. But leadership training was something I knew about and loved from my time in the Marines. That actually got my attention.

George gave me his business card, and I told him I'd think about it. It was an interesting and certainly unexpected proposal, but I had just taken a job at the shipyard and was hardly in a place to tell my new boss, "Hey, I'd like to leave at 3 p.m. every day and have Fridays and Mondays off to go coach football."

Denise had also just started a new job, working at the Bremerton School District in human resources, so I asked her what she knew of this Smiling George Duarte guy and his proposal. She was excited by the idea and told me to pray about it. I said a quick prayer, as is my habit when it comes to praying, and then fully intended to put it from my mind in order to quickly work my way up the ladder at the shipyard.

Little did I know that Smiling George Duarte would begin to routinely follow me on my daily runs. Every few days, I'd see him as I ran past the high school while he was driving into work. He'd honk his horn, roll down his window, and ask me if I'd considered his offer to come coach. I figured after being rebuffed a few times, he'd get the hint that I wasn't really interested—but for *two years*, he kept asking me.

At the shipyard, I had been hired as a pipe fitter. I had retired from the Marines as a mechanic and was overly qualified to connect pipes and mop floors, but I loved the mindless work. About six to eight months into my new job, my boss came over while I was sweating like crazy. I was wearing a Marine Corps shirt, so he asked what I had done in the Corps. I told him that I was a senior enlisted guy who ran a transportation division of engineering and mechanic shops. I had done quality assurance as the director of maintenance for years. My boss told me that the shipyard needed someone to run quality assurance and offered me a promotion.

It typically takes years to earn these types of promotions, but I got one before I even officially finished my initial training, jumping from Working Grade (WG) Level 1 to a WG8 within a year. I was then transferred from the nuclear division to the engineering side of the shipyard, where I became a General Salaried (GS) employee. I kept getting promoted up the chain of command, until two years later, I was transferred back to the nuclear side, where I oversaw a department and could choose my own hours. By then, each time that Smiling George Duarte would roll down his window on my run and ask me to coach football, I was actually in a place to begin considering the offer. Just a coincidence, I'm sure.

I took George up on an invitation to meet the Bremerton High coaching team and observe a practice. I quickly noticed there was no clear chain of command between the players and the three team captains: The coaches seemed to be doing a lot of the jobs that the team captains could have and should have been doing. I told George that the team could be run much more efficiently. It would also free the coaches up to spend more time coaching if they had their captains do the menial tasks like overseeing the locker room.

While I was happy to give my two cents free of charge and continue working at the shipyard, he doubled down on his efforts to recruit me as an assistant coach under Bremerton's brand-new head coach. Even though seeing firsthand how I could contribute to the team made the offer more tempting, I knew that coaching was going to be a major time commitment.

I had been too busy playing Marine to be present in my only son's life while he was growing up, and I didn't want to make that mistake again now that I was finally married to Denise. She, however, was quick to point out that this was an opportunity to be a father figure to the guys on the football team, many of whom were from single-parent homes without a positive male presence in their lives.

I was interviewed on a Friday. The school had been interviewing lots of other, way more experienced coaches for the job but offered me the assistant coaching position on the spot. I was still on the fence about committing to the team and asked for the weekend to think about it. I went home to find a note from Denise taped to the fridge telling me she would be home late from a school board meeting.

I sat down on the living room couch and started channel surfing, finally stumbling across a football movie called *Facing the Giants*. I had just recommitted my life to God and considered myself a baby Christian. For most of my life, I had believed in God, but I had also gone through periods of backsliding. This time, for the first time, I had told God I was "all in."

As I watched the movie, it felt like God was reaching through the TV with His invisible hand, grabbing me by the heart, and just squeezing it. Not to hurt it, but to embrace it. I just melted right there in my living room into a big blubbering mess. Here I was, a career Marine, sobbing on the floor over a movie. Marines don't cry! Yet as I watched the scenes where the football coach explained his new team philosophy and made the kids do the death crawl, I realized that God was calling me to coach football. I fell to my knees and prayed right then and there, "God, I hear You loud and clear. I'm in, and win or lose, I'm going to give You thanks after every game."

I don't exactly know where the idea to do it on the fifty-yard line came from, but that was the mental image I had in my head when I made my vow, and I wasn't going to question it.

. . .

What many may not realize is that my habit of praying a thirty-second prayer on the fifty-yard line was a non-event for years. After a football game, while the players were celebrating or singing the fight song, I would walk out to the middle of the field, take a knee and say my quick "Thank You" to God, and that was that. Eventually some of the players started coming out with me. I didn't want them praying with me, and I told them so.

They said, "Coach, we think it's cool what you're doing, and we want to join."

I reluctantly shrugged and said, "It's a free country."

Praying during a football game was not some novel thing. At some point during my eight seasons as an assistant coach, every member of our coaching staff prayed in the locker room before a game, from our head coach on down—including my Buddhist friend and fellow assistant coach, Pappy Boynton. Nobody complained about the pregame prayer. It was tradition. People have been praying at high school football games for the protection of the players and as a way to give thanks to God since the first pigskin was passed. Ours was not formal or specific to a certain faith. It was just an acknowledgment of God before the game. Nobody cared if you bowed your head and closed your eyes, or if you thought about where you were going to take your girlfriend to eat after the game. It was a tradition we all abided by.

Similarly, my prayer was my own personal tradition that my players decided to participate in. Even Pappy came out to pray with me, and he's a devout Buddhist! Eventually, my players started inviting players from the opposing teams to join us on the fifty-yard line. The quarterbacks of both teams would give me their helmets to raise up as I gave my prayer of thanks. Oftentimes, it was no more than "God, thank You for these guys, thank You for the game of football. You're awesome. Amen." For eight seasons I did this and, while many players and coaches would join me from my team and others, many opted not to. I never had a problem with either choice. I just wanted to do *my* prayer and then celebrate with my team if we won or encourage them if we lost.

In 2014, after one particular game, the opposing team's head coach called the Bremerton High School principal to tell him he had seen me praying on the field and thought it was a really cool thing to do. No one ever told me which coach that was, but the principal got nervous that we could land in legal hot water if this continued.

A few days later, the school district issued a directive telling me to stop praying with the kids. Since I never wanted to pray with the kids in the first place, I was more than willing to comply. I asked if I could still do my prayer at the fifty-yard line after the game by myself, and the district reiterated that as long as I didn't pray with the kids, I was in the clear. So I kept praying. The kids didn't understand why—if it was a free country, as I'd told them—they could no longer join me on the field for the prayer.

I can still remember the smell of them surrounding me as I closed my eyes to take a knee. Even though I had explicitly told them not to pray with me, the odor of a dozen sweaty football players gave away their defiant positions pretty quickly. When I opened my eyes to see the new athletic director talking with the head coach, it was clear that I was in trouble.

When I showed up at the office the next day, the other coaches were noticeably peeved.

"Way to go, Kennedy," the head coach barked. "The new athletic director wants to talk to you about the prayer thing."

"What about it?" I asked.

"You can't do it anymore."

"What do you mean I can't do it anymore?"

The other coaches told me I had gotten everyone in trouble over it, and I could be fired if I didn't comply. I took Pappy aside. "Pappy, you don't think—they can't fire me over this, can they?"

In my head, I was thinking there was no way they could. The Christian part of me reasoned that it was all a big misunderstanding.

I would just put my foot down harder with the kids about not praying with me. But the other part of me—the Marine part—was angry. It was one thing to tell me I couldn't pray with the kids, but now they were telling me *I couldn't pray at all?* And if I did keep praying, I could lose my job?

"What are you going to do?" Pappy asked me.

He must have seen the Marine side take over and a defiant look settle over my face because he started warning me, "Don't do it, man. It's not worth it."

To me, it *was* worth it. I've never been the most moral or ethical guy, but I have always stood by my principles.

"You're going to do it, aren't you?" Pappy sighed.

"I can't promise anything," I responded.

In that moment, in all honesty, I didn't know what I was going to do. When the game ended that Friday night in double overtime, it looked like there was not going to be enough time to do the prayer. I think the athletic director was about to breathe a sigh of relief. He even came up to me, put his arm around my shoulders and said, "Boy, we really dodged a bullet there."

There were back-to-back games scheduled that day, and as we were heading off the field, the players for the next game were already pouring onto it to hurry through their warmups. But as we were returning to the locker room, one of the players from the *opposing* team came up to me and asked, "Coach, would you use my helmet for your prayer?"

I didn't give it a second thought. I couldn't say "no" now. I took his helmet and ran onto the field to do my prayer. It was really quick because we had to get the heck out of there.

As I jogged back to the locker room, none of the other coaches would make eye contact with me. The new athletic director had disappeared, and Pappy was standing in the corner shaking his head, smiling with his *Kennedy's gonna do what Kennedy's gonna do* expression. The head coach silently mouthed to me, "They're going to fire you."

Oh crap, what did I just do?

. . .

A sick feeling took over my gut as we got onto the bus to drive back to Bremerton. I went on Facebook and posted, "I think I just got fired from coaching for praying."

Early the next morning, my phone started blowing up with calls, texts, and emails. I jumped up, wondering if someone had died, and happened to pick up as a friend was calling.

She began yelling, "Joe, you're on TV! They're talking about you on the national news."

I thought she was pulling my leg, but Denise's phone had been blowing up almost as much as mine. She flipped on the TV and, sure enough, my picture was plastered on the national news regarding my Facebook post from the night before. I still have no idea how that post went viral. (I'm sure it's all just a coincidence, right?)

Denise and I went into panic mode. As the HR supervisor for the Bremerton School District, she was getting calls from major news outlets asking for a comment because of my post. We called Aaron, the superintendent, to find out if I still had my job.

"Aaron," I asked, "What's going on? Am I fired?"

Graciously, Aaron talked us down.

"I'm the only person who can fire you," he said. "And no, you're not fired."

"So, what do we do?" I asked, terrified by how fast this had spun out of control.

Aaron promised us we'd sort everything out on Monday.

The school district's lawyer began an investigation and started interviewing all the coaches on the staff. Denise and I steered clear of social media and avoided phone calls as best we could. I started getting hate mail and death threats from random strangers. People everywhere were asking me if I was going to pray that coming Friday night at the game. Everything was being blown way out of proportion.

Once again, the Christian and the Marine in me began to wrestle with each other. I asked Pappy one day after practice, "What should I do on Friday night?"

"You really want my advice?" he asked.

"Always."

"You already know what you're going to do."

"No, I don't!" I exclaimed, thinking he was trying one of his Buddhist Jedi mind tricks on me.

"Think about it," he went on. "You've got to do what you've got to do as a man in this situation. Isn't that what we always tell the kids?"

"Well, yeah," I replied.

"So, what are you worried about?" he asked in his typical dry manner.

I wish I could say I knew right then and there what I was going to do, but I was up all night long that Thursday, praying and wrestling with my options.

When I showed up at the school the next day, thousands of people were camped out, waiting for the game. There were news cameras all over. A dozen of the local Satanic Temple members came out in black robes with hoods and horns. Christians were protesting with signs and crosses. On the Bremerton Walk of Fame—a series of boulders etched with the names and stats of former standout football players dating back for decades—one kid stood holding a giant cross and leading a crowd in chanting, "Je-sus! Je-sus! Je-sus!" Even though there were people on both sides of the issue, it seemed like most of the ones who turned up to that game were actually supporting me!

Police showed up to control the crowds because of the chaos. I was overwhelmed. I know the other coaches were, too. The only people enjoying the chaos were the kids who were showing off for the cameras and telling their moms "hi" on TV.

After the game, people flooded onto the field. The kids came over and handed me their helmets at the fifty-yard line. I don't remember exactly what I said, but I was very careful to not pray. Regardless, at the end, many people still yelled "Amen!" Cameras were being shoved in my face while people were waving flags, and I just wanted to get the heck off the field. The crowds stayed until almost midnight.

The other coaches and I got the kids back to the locker room. None of the coaches were talking. There was a silence so tense it was like being back in a fighting hole in Kuwait after we got word that enemy soldiers were walking through our position.

I had always made a habit of staying at the school until the last kid left. Sometimes we'd go out for a bite after the game, but that night, I just wanted to get home. I got into my truck, and this nagging feeling began to eat away inside my gut. I felt like I'd done something wrong.

The closer I got to my house, the stronger this feeling became—as if I had committed some great sin. I couldn't stand it. Here I was, always telling the kids to stand up for what they believed in, even if it wasn't popular, yet I had just copped out of saying my prayer because of the media chaos. I had broken my promise to God—the only real promise I'd ever made Him.

I turned my truck around and drove all the way back to the high school. As I pulled up to the stadium, I saw that the lights were still on and the camera crews and reporters were almost all packed up for the night. I bargained with God to let me pray from the safety of my parked truck, but He wouldn't let me off the hook. That feeling was still eating away at my gut.

I asked God to help me get to the fifty-yard line without getting spotted by the cameras. I snuck down to the field; it was completely empty. I went to take my knee and have my moment alone with God—and then I lost my cool and started yelling at Him.

"Why are You doing this?" I cried out. "God, I need to know right here and right now if this is You or if this is me and my own pride. You've got to help me, because I don't know how to handle this."

I didn't want to give up, but everything I'd worked so hard for with the team—the character-building and mentoring, not to mention the relationship I'd built with these guys!—was all hanging in the balance, and I needed to be sure that my pride was not getting in the way.

"God, please. Just give me a sign. Show me something," I prayed. As I said "amen," I went to punch the ground. As soon as my hand made contact with the field, all the stadium lights went out.

I was alone on the field in the pitch dark with nothing but the moonlight when suddenly, I was overcome with laughter because God had given me my sign: It was not my pride; it was Him. All I could do was laugh, because I knew in that moment that He had my back regardless of what came next. I told Him, "I will never ever turn my back on You." Immediately, that guilty feeling I had been wrestling with went away, and my conscience was clean again.

The following week, the school's communication systems crashed from the overload of people calling and emailing—not to complain about my prayer, but to complain about the way the school district responded to my prayer. But the school doubled down: I received two more directives from the district telling me that in addition to not praying with the kids, my options now were to stop praying on the field altogether or start praying in a closet in the locker room by myself.

That really made me mad. I felt that was a blatant violation of my First Amendment rights. I didn't have a problem with not praying with the kids, but I had a *big* problem with being told to hide in a closet to pray like I was being sent to time-out. I wasn't about to do that.

Shortly thereafter, I was suspended from coaching. It was clear that the only reason was my prayer; it had nothing to do with my ability or dedication as a coach. I was being singled out and punished because of my religious expression.

Around that time, lawyers began to approach me about representing me in court. Though I never wanted to get lawyers involved, by then, I realized I was being discriminated against and if I didn't do something, I would definitely lose my job.

. . .

My last game was rather anticlimactic. The media crowds had died down, and it was the first normal-feeling game we'd had that season. We were playing North Mason High School and, when I went out to do my prayer during the Bremerton fight song, nobody from my own team joined.

At the end of the school year, where I once had nothing but glowing reviews from my supervisors, this time my evaluations showed low marks in every area—but the only thing that had changed was the school's response to my prayer. There had been no change in my coaching style or my dedication to the team. Even my prayer had not changed from previous years, except for the fact that it had become a media event.

Despite my efforts to comply with the school district's directives, they had suspended me from coaching the last few games of the season. The district even put a sign on the field reading "No Unauthorized Personnel Beyond This Point." That was never there before;

it was directed at me. Being a spectator for those last games just about killed me. I didn't want to sit in the stands and draw attention to myself, but I couldn't *not* show up for my guys, so I stood as far away from everyone as possible to watch. If my players blew a play or had an amazing one, I couldn't be there to comfort them or celebrate with them on the sidelines.

After I was suspended, the school district created a new policy of having all coaches reapply at the end of every school year. That's when I knew my coaching career was over.

Contrary to rumors, my wife did not fire me. As head of HR, technically that would have been her job, but thankfully, the superintendent spared her from having to do that. It's funny, though, because I did help that rumor along. When I later began traveling around the country to speak about my case and Denise was sitting in the audience, I would point her out and ask, "Why'd you fire me, honey?" She always *hated* that, even though it would get a big laugh everyone else.

What really happened was that when I got my 2015 year-end evaluation back, it was simply stamped with big, red block letters that read: DO NOT REHIRE. This ensured that no one, under any circumstances, could ever rehire me within the Bremerton School District, no matter how many applications I put in or if the leadership changed in the future. I would never be allowed to set foot back on the football field unless the courts ruled in my favor.

My coaching career was over, but my fight had just begun. Thankfully, fighting was something I knew how to do. Looking back at my crazy life, I now see how God used it all as preparation for that precise moment, and I was prepared to fight to the end.

CHAPTER 2

HIGH SCHOOL FOOTBALL IS NOTHING LIKE MARINE CORPS FOOTBALL

Before coaching at Bremerton, my experience with football had been limited to playing with a team of maniacal Marines known as the Bone Crushers. Our whole mission objective in playing football was to put people out of the game and send them to the doc. It was an unorganized, beat-the-living-crap-out-of-each-other kind of game. This wasn't regular football. This was *Marine Corps* football, and it was awesome.

The Bone Crushers got started when I was stationed in Hawaii in the late '90s, early 2000s. A new football league was being created within the Corps. Unlike your typical eleven-man football, this was more arena style. Each team had only eight men. I played defensive end, a position for which I was very much undersized, but because I was a martial arts instructor and experienced wrestler, I knew how to manipulate a body. I understood people's center of gravity and turned out to be naturally good in that position.

I was one of the oldest players in the league. There were only three other people my age—all senior enlisted guys, which made the age difference really noticeable—but I have always felt like a big kid trapped in an adult's body.

I'll never forget our first game. I was so amped up that I was clenching my fists as hard as I could when one of the other guys on the defensive line started shouting at me.

"Kennedy!"

I was in the zone. I didn't have time to chit-chat. But he wouldn't stop.

"KENNEDY!"

After a few times of him calling to me, I looked over at him. He was pointing at my hands with a horrified look on his face. I looked down at my hands and realized I had ripped all the fingernails off one of them. My hand was just dripping blood. I hadn't even noticed because the battlefield adrenaline was so high. I was ready to fight!

The other team was visibly rattled by this. A normal human would have called a time-out and tended to the wound, probably with an apology. Not me. I reveled in the pain and psychological terror it inflicted on the opponent. Afterall, this wasn't going to be some sweet, recreational weekend game. This was war!

Ironically, I didn't care about winning or losing. The only thing I cared about was sacking the quarterback. I played on their blindside and would just level those guys. It may sound twisted, but there was no better feeling. Especially when the quarterback was a commanding officer.

Just before joining the Bone Crushers, I had been promoted to gunnery sergeant, which meant I was directly over a thousand Marines in my battalion. That put a target on my back on the field. This was the other team's chance to come at me with everything they could, but I could always feel them coming. I credit it to the heightened situational awareness I developed while living on the streets as a teenager—you become hyper-aware of everything. I always had my head on a swivel. It was like a sixth sense. They would try again and again to flatten me, but I would simply sidestep them. It annoyed the crap out of them. Those were some of the best times—Marines being Marines on the gridiron.

I often get asked if I applied anything from the Bone Crushers to coaching high school football. That question never fails to make me laugh because, in terms of how we actually played the game, most of our strategy would have created a whole different set of lawsuits than my prayer did.

I was never an X's and O's player. I didn't study the plays or the strategy as much as I studied my position, but that is how I coached. I never worried about what the guy next to me was doing on the field. That was his job. I was laser focused on what *my* role was. Sometimes, I would pull one of my players out of the game and have him watch someone else run a play in his position so he could see it from my point of view. Inevitably, he would see lanes open up that he couldn't see when he was in the middle of the situation. He would then turn to me and say, "Why the heck didn't the other guy do this or that?" And he would have a new understanding of how to better do his job.

I also instilled the mindset in my players that football is like war. When you're on the field, your job is to protect your men and accomplish the objective of moving the ball down the field to score touchdowns. You do not pick up your opponent when they've fallen; you knock the crap out of them. Only after it's over do you go shake hands and acknowledge a battle well fought. I was probably the biggest jerk because of my no-mercy strategy, but I wanted to teach these guys that, when they were in the middle of the battle, they were to be fully committed to what was going on. Only *afterward* could you flip the switch and become a normal human again.

Most of what I brought to the field as a coach, however, was respect, leadership, and discipline. Respect was one of the biggest things I tried to instill in my guys. From the first day I set foot on the field as a coach, I never let anybody call me "Joe" or "Kennedy" or "Bud" or "Hey, you." It was always "yes, Coach," or "no, Coach." They would never address me as anything else. I was very formal about the title. I don't think they even realized what a big thing that was, because I just set it up that way from the beginning.

My players worried about my opinion of them more than anyone else's. When they screwed up on the field, they would look over at me to gauge my reaction. I never had to yell at them. The other coaches loved to yell and curse, but I never had to. I would just shake my head a little and give them a look, and they would know they had messed up. They'd come talk to me about how to fix it, and we would work through it together.

Beyond respect for the coaches and other players on the team, it was very important to me to teach these young men how to respect women. When I started traveling with the team to away games, the cheerleaders would ride with us on the buses. I was amazed at how many of the football players would push their way onto the bus ahead of the cheerleaders, use foul language in front of them, and saw little need to control their gross bodily fumes while they were around. I set up protocols dictating that not only would the guys wait until every last cheerleader was on the bus before they began to board, but they also had to help carry their bags and load them into the undercarriage to and from games. They had to watch their language on the bus and act the way they would if they were around their grandmothers. Pretty soon, it became habitual. (Plus, the buses smelled a lot better.)

When I heard from a kid's mom that he had disrespected her, I would call a time-out, pull that kid out of the game, and make him go over to the sideline and do jumping jacks while shouting, "I love you, Mom! I'm sorry, Mom!" over and over again until all the players got it through their thick heads that they had to treat their parents with respect.

Every year, I'd make the players spend time with someone they never would have hung out with ordinarily—the kids they thought were *uncool,* and often bullied. I had zero tolerance for bullying because I had been bullied, and I had also been a bully. I must have apologized about a million times to the kids I bullied in my school days. As a result, as an adult I was now overly sensitive to the subject. I had a strict antibullying policy with my players. I wanted them to get to know the uncool and unpopular kids and see that they were really no different than anybody else. Most of the time, my guys would become friends with those kids and report back to me that they learned something cool about them. It made them learn that their preconceived judgments of others were often incorrect. It was more important to me that my guys learned how to be decent human beings than great football players. Football was a brief season in their lives; courtesy and respect were traits they would use forever as adults.

Leadership was the second big thing that I focused on. I wanted to train these young men to become leaders, so I put together a program called "Corporals to Captains." After practice and on weekends, I would teach them about leadership. A lot of what I taught was based on what I had learned in the Marines.

I believe that hierarchy simplifies everything and makes teams more efficient. One of the first things I implemented was making use of our team captains. Instead of making the coaches lead warmups and cooldowns, or ensure that the locker room was clean after each practice, we trained the captains to lead these tasks. The captains would set up the weights and call the water breaks, leaving the coaches more time to run plays and review defense and offense.

Instead of running practice like boot camp where the coaches, like drill instructors, controlled everything and even told you when to breathe, I started running the team like an NCO program[1] that delegated responsibility down the chain of command. Some of the coaches didn't like this at first because they liked having the control. Coaches can be control freaks, but once they realized that it was much easier not to have to worry about the little stuff because they could rely on the team captains, they got on board. Instead of yelling at the whole team when something went wrong, we would talk to our captains and they would pass the message down the hierarchy to the team.

With discipline, I tried to give my guys challenges that pushed them and made them work together. Anyone can run laps or hit the weight room. That's boring. The players hated it and just wanted to be done. So I tried to think of more creative endurance-building exercises. I would set up obstacle courses and make the guys run while holding forty-five-pound weight plates out in front of them like steering wheels. We would go on long runs with random squat or push-up intervals while trolling the nearby high schools. We would go out to the military base and do Marine for a Day training. While the rest of the coaches would sit and watch, one of the other assistant coaches and I would compete against the kids on obstacle courses and combat courses. Anytime I could turn something into a game or a competition, I did. Plus, because I firmly believe in leading by example (also, because I'm a big kid), I would join in, which made it even more fun. Everyone took the challenge more seriously when they had the chance to beat me.

As a result of the unorthodox training, we had one of the best-conditioned teams in our district. This was always a big confidence

---

1 Non-Commissioned Officer leadership program—the first step in the Marines' officer leadership training curriculum

booster to the guys because they could look back and say, "Hey, remember when we did that two-mile run while carrying a fifty-pound weight? That was crazy!" They felt tough and proud, and because they all shared the same experience and had to encourage each other to complete the task, it built a stronger team spirit.

One year, we had a lineman who easily weighed four hundred pounds. He was in incredibly good shape—a giant, strong kid. If anybody got within arm's length of him on the field, he would level them. He was also just a good, sweet kid with a heart of gold. Everybody loved him.

One of the funniest challenges was when we were at the Marine base doing a combat readiness test and we had to do a buddy carry. We had a bunch of strong kids on the team, but nobody could carry that lineman. I often say that there's a line between brave and stupid, and I don't know where that line is. After teasing my guys about not being able to carry that lineman, I told him to get on my back. He hoisted himself up; it was like carrying a four-hundred-pound water balloon. His whole weight seemed to just fall off my backside. I could not get my balance right to save my life, so I ended up getting two players to hold the kid's arms and two more to hold his legs in place so I could hold his body. The six of us ran the entire obstacle course together. It was hilarious and so much fun. The kids told that story for months afterward.

In addition to the physical toughness, I taught mental toughness. I used a lot of psychological warfare tactics with my players, to which they were oblivious. I had a lot of fun coming up with ways to psych the team up before games. One week, we had a big game coming up against our rival, Kingston High School. They had T-shirts that showed their school as a big shark eating little minnows with all the other high school teams' names in the area. I bought one of those T-shirts and showed it to my guys.

"You see this? This is what Kingston thinks of us," I told them. "They think you're just a tiny minnow and they're gonna come into our home and kick our butts. Are you guys gonna let that happen?" They got so fired up, "No, Coach!" Our offense and defensive lines had a tug-of-war as they shredded that shirt.

Another time, we were about to play North Kitsap, and I bought a ton of glitter in their school colors and dumped it all over the field. I had posters made with Kitsap's mascot stomping on ours, and put them up all over the stadium. I told our players that the North Kitsap players had done all of it. That lit a fire under their butts for game night. Nobody was going to come into our house and disrespect our team! It was so much fun to think of creative ways to get inside our team's head and get them psyched for battle, and they had no idea that I was constantly messing with them.

But when it came to handling conflict, I always preferred a direct approach. If two guys were having some sort of beef with each other, I would separate them from the rest of the team and make them work together. If they were too fired up, I'd let them duke it out. It made the other coaches nervous at first, but my thinking was that they were already in full pads, so how much harm could they really do? Once they knocked each other around a little bit and the initial steam wore off, they'd settle down and I could bring them together to talk. I'd sit down with both of them and get them to tell me what was wrong. Sometimes one would answer, "So-and-so just slept with my girlfriend."

"Yup, that's a problem. She's obviously not your girlfriend anymore."

They would get butthurt a bit over that, but I'd explain, "It doesn't seem like she has a lot of respect for you, if she did that, so you're probably better off without her, don't you think?"

They'd think it over and come to the realization that it wasn't worth fighting over the girl anymore. Not every issue was so cut and dried, but most of the ones that came up between players could be solved by letting them burn off some steam and then talk about it face-to-face like men. I didn't accept passive aggression. Life is conflict. Conflict is unavoidable. Better to deal with it head on and move past it than let it fester and create unnecessary drama. Too many people these days are afraid of conflict when it is a natural part of life. You are not always going to agree with everybody on every issue. Feelings are bound to get hurt, misunderstandings are going to happen, balls are going to get dropped. You have to communicate, be honest with each other, and then figure out a way to move past the issue—and you cannot do that unless you are willing to engage in conflict.

One of the last big issues I would have to guide my players through was handling disappointment. One incident that immediately comes to mind was when a player completely blew a play to lose the game. That's a difficult thing to deal with as a young man—knowing that you let your team down and cost everyone a victory—but it happens.

This happened to a kid I called Gatorade. Washington is often rainy, but for that particular game, the sky had really opened up. The field had completely turned to mud, and everyone's uniforms were so dirty you couldn't tell the two teams apart anymore. A big scrum had formed around the twenty-yard line, and Gatorade was looking for an opening to push through so he could run the ball. Gatorade finally got free and got all the way from the ten- to the one-yard line when he lost the ball. The conditions were so wet and muddy that it popped right out of his hands and into the hands of some third-string guy from the opposing team (who must have just been put into the game because his uniform was still clean). He caught the ball, and both he and Gatorade were so surprised that they stared at each other a moment before the kid took off running to score a ninety-nine-yard touchdown to win the game. It was a freak play, but Gatorade took it really hard.

I took him aside after the game, and he kept apologizing and beating himself up about it. Had *Ted Lasso* been around at that time, I'd have borrowed his famous goldfish speech, but instead, I told Gatorade that he had to leave that play and that whole game in the past. Yeah, it sucked, but the only thing that mattered now was the next play and the next game. You cannot let past failures and mistakes define your future, no matter how big they may seem. You have to leave the past in the past. I told him that nobody besides him and the kid who scored that epic touchdown (and now all of you reading this) would ever remember that play. Once he finally changed his mindset, he went on to set every record that season and is now immortalized on the Bremerton Walk of Fame.

I was always proud of my players. They were like my kids. To be honest, I was a much better coach than I ever was a father to my own kid. In a way, I viewed coaching as an opportunity to atone for that. Having grown up an unwanted kid shuffled around through the foster care system, I never had anyone really teach me how to be a man. By the time I had a kid of my own, I was too busy playing Marine to really be the father he deserved. When I became old enough to finally figure out what it meant to be a man, I was in a place to help instill those principles into my football players. I still stay in touch with many of my players. I've even officiated a wedding for one of them. I've held their newborn kids and grieved with them at their parents' funerals, all because I poured into them and made them feel like they mattered in the ways I always wished someone had for me when I was their age.

CHAPTER 3

THE KID NOBODY WANTED

I never really had a family until I married Denise. I was given up for adoption at birth. My biological mom never even knew if I was a boy or a girl. She was told that the family adopting me lived on a farm and was financially well-off and loving.

That was a lie.

My adopted dad was a nine-to-five guy who worked at the Navy Shipyard. He never would have stood out in a crowd. His one pride was belonging to the Knights of Columbus, which I'm pretty sure he used to escape the house. She was the overbearing wife who desperately wanted kids.

At the time they adopted me and my older sister, they thought they couldn't conceive. That changed when I was about three years old, and they began quickly popping out kids of their own. Suddenly, it felt like my older sister and I were no longer needed. It didn't help that, admittedly, I was an absolute demon child, always fighting and getting into trouble. I'm not talking about the type of fighting that begins with, "Mom! He called me a doo-doo head!" and ends with some crying, screaming, and being sent to time-out in a corner, either. I'm talking about knock-down, drag-out fights.

One of my earliest memories is of a big fight I had with my adopted older sister after I tried to hit her with a machete. I wound up getting the worse end of that deal, suffering a few broken ribs in the process.

When I was about nine or ten, she and I got into another big fight. I'm sure I hadn't been doing anything even remotely annoying when she chose to throw a shoe at me. My reflexes kicked in and I managed to duck out of the way. The shoe sailed past and hit my dad's prized fifty-gallon aquarium instead.

There were only two things my dad ever truly loved in life: photography and his fish. I had long since destroyed all his cameras through my curiosity to discover how they worked. That day, we destroyed his fish. The shoe crashed through the aquarium glass, sending the fish cascading in a waterfall onto the linoleum floor. My sister desperately tried to scoop the dying fish up in her hands while I grabbed every towel in the house to sop up the water. I think that was the only time I ever saw my dad cry. I actually did feel really bad about that one, because I thought his aquarium was pretty cool, too. He was heartbroken.

In hindsight, I'm sure I acted out because I subconsciously sensed I was no longer wanted. But when you're a little kid, you don't understand why Mom and Dad are suddenly paying so much attention to their own babies and not you.

As a result, I hated their first biological child, Gina, and picked on her mercilessly. One day, Gina wanted to come with us to play with some of the neighborhood kids. Even though I told her, "Okay," I had other plans. I locked her in our goat pen while the rest of us went to play and left her there for hours. All the neighborhood kids called her Goat from then on.

The only one of my siblings I actually liked was Sharon. She was so tiny. I would actually hold her and sing to her. The other siblings would pick on her because she was the baby until Timmy came along, but I protected her.

Because I had undiagnosed ADD/ADHD, I had limitless energy that my parents did not know how to deal with. One time, my older sister and I thought it would be funny to prank-call the fire department. After several minutes of "You do it," and "No, *you* do it!" I picked up the phone and dialed 911.

"Fire! Fire! Fire!" I yelled, and then immediately hung up, giggling.

To our surprise, ten minutes later, the fire truck arrived at our house. Apparently, dispatch had traced the call. My parents were across the street visiting our neighbors, but I knew they would be furious when they found out what we'd done. As they rushed home to meet the firefighters, I ran into my room and hid under the bed. I was so scared, I crawled up into the undercarriage of my box spring mattress and was holding onto the metal support beams for dear life. From my hiding spot, I saw my parents' feet enter my room, followed by the firefighters' big, heavy boots.

"JOSEPH KENNEDY, come out this instant!" my mom shouted.

Of course, I was not about to listen. My older sister began ratting me out, saying that it had all been my idea, and I had been the one who made the call. Even though she was telling the truth, it made me mad that she had tattled on me! I couldn't help myself as I protested my innocence, giving away my position in the process as I yelled, "Nuh-uh! She's lying!"

One of the firefighters stooped down to pull me out from under the bed, but I had a death grip on the metal rails. It took four firefighters to take my bed apart and get me out from under it. My mom was mortified. Even after they got me out, I wrestled to get away from their strong grip. They scolded me, and even tried to scare me from ever prank-calling them again by threatening to throw me in jail.

Shortly afterward, we moved; my parents were building a new house to hold their now seven children. When we went to check on the progress of the house, a kid from down the street walked up to me and demanded to know, "What are you doing here?"

I told him we were going to be moving in.

"Oh yeah? This is *my* neighborhood," he said.

"Cool," I replied, unfazed. "Wanna go throw rocks?"

That was the beginning of my lifelong friendship with Ty, whom I often refer to as my brother. We had every adventure under the sun. We had BB gun wars in the woods. We built BMX racetracks. We collected aluminum cans and traded them for nickels to buy Gobstoppers. I never had any money as a kid, but Ty's parents always saw to it that I was taken care of and would give me a place to stay when things got bad at my house. At mealtimes, I was always at their house because his mom would cook and the entire family would sit together for dinner. To this day, I refer to Ty's parents as Mom and Dad, and I still go see them. They're my family.

Ty had a younger sister, Audrey—who, like Sharon, was a really small kid. Audrey was always getting picked on, and we felt very protective of her. I hated kids who picked on other kids who were smaller than they were. It made my blood boil. One time, while we were playing, a neighborhood kid punched Audrey in the face. Her nose started bleeding, and she began crying. Ty and I took off after that kid like guided missiles. We were going to make him pay. He ran into his home and hid behind his mom, crying like a coward, "Mom, they're going to kill me!" We tore in right behind him, totally barging into the house uninvited. I grabbed him from behind his mom and started punching him; his mom grabbed me by the throat and lifted me off the floor, screaming, "Who do you think you are! You think you can just come in my house and assault my son?"

She was hysterical. She had me in a death grip by the neck, choking me. I was a really small kid, and she held me by the throat with my feet lifted off the floor. Ty told me later that I was turning almost blue. I struggled for air, thinking I was going to die. Ty, who *never cussed* in front of adults *ever*, cussed at this lady to break her attention away from choking the life out of me.

"Put him down, *witch*!" he yelled.[1]

It worked. She and I both looked at him, mouths agape. There was an awkward moment where I could see the revelation dawn on that lady's face that she was killing me. She threw me to the ground and kicked us out of the house. Her son never messed with Audrey again.

Aside from that scuffle, the first real fight I ever got into was with Ty. It was over a girl. But not just any girl: *Denise.*

I had gotten expelled from the school that Ty went to because I put Ex-Lax in a teacher's coffee. When I got off the bus from my new school, Ty could barely contain himself with the news that he was in love.

"Joey, the most beautiful girl just moved in down the street. Go tell her that I want to marry her."

Even as a kid, I always loved girls. I wanted to see this new girl that Ty was starry-eyed over. We rode our BMX bikes down the street. Ty pulled over a few houses away from our target and hid behind the bushes, entrusting me to find out if this girl liked him back. I went up to her house, and that's when I saw her.

She was sitting on the front stoop in her little dress, playing in the dirt, humming to herself. As I came up her front walkway and she

---

1 That's not an exact quote, but you get the idea.

looked up, the world seemed to stop like one of those cheesy Hallmark movie, slow-motion scenes. Her dark hair was blowing in the breeze, and she looked up at me with the biggest, most beautiful brown eyes I had ever seen in my life. Even at nine years old, she completely took my breath away.

"Can I help you?" she asked innocently.

"I want to marry you," I said breathlessly.

In what seemed like slow motion, I saw a look of horror cross her face.

"MOM!?" she cried out as she ran to the door before calling back to me, "You're creepy!"

She slammed the door in my face, but I didn't care. I was in love.

After a minute, Ty ventured out from his hiding place to come check on the situation.

"So, what did she say?"

"I didn't ask."

"What do you mean you didn't ask!"

"I'm going to marry her," I said.

"No, you're not!" he retorted, getting defensive.

"Yes, I am," I said, fully convinced that I had just met the love of my life.

My reverie was broken by a fist to the face. Ty's mom had to break us up by spraying us with ice-cold water from the hose. We made up pretty quickly, as kids do, but it became an ongoing battle between us to see who could win Denise's heart. (Spoiler alert: I eventually won).

Every day after school, we would ride our bikes down to Denise's house and do BMX tricks. It got to the point where her mom would see us coming and yell, "Denise, the vultures are here again!"

Denise eventually became friends with us, and the three of us spent countless days together. It was heaven compared to my home life.

. . .

Though I loved my fourth-grade teacher and did my best to behave in her class, I *hated* my fifth-grade teacher. I started skipping school regularly to go hustle drunks down at the pool hall. I was always looking for ways to make money, and I would ask the pool hall patrons if they wanted to play a game. The bet was for one dollar. Most of them thought they could easily beat a ten-year-old at a game of pool. What they didn't realize was that I was the perfect height to see the pool table. I got good at pool really quickly. The lady who owned the pool hall told me she could get in trouble for letting me hang out there, but when I told her that I'd only find somewhere else to hang out, she decided it was better for her to keep an eye on me than someone at one of the other bars in town. She would cook me breakfast and let me hustle her clientele.

Every now and again I would lose to one of the morning drunks, but most of the time, I would make a couple bucks. I had a good run at the pool hall until one guy lost fifty bucks to me. I beat him game after game after game. He got so mad! He couldn't believe he was losing to a kid. The more we played, the angrier he got. When it came time to pay up, he flat-out refused to give me the money. I cussed him out, which did not help my case. He called me a foul-mouthed little turd and tried to grab me. When the owner came over to intervene, he threatened to call the cops on her for letting a snot-nosed kid in her bar.

After that, she wouldn't let me come around anymore. With nowhere else to hang out, that's when I really started getting in trouble at school for fighting.

There must be something psychologically wrong with me, because I have always loved a fight. Win or lose, I love the physical contact of one-on-one fighting. In high school, I found legitimate ways to feed that passion through wrestling. In the Marine Corps, I took all sorts of martial arts classes, but in elementary school and junior high, I would pick random fights with random kids for the fun of it.

In fourth grade, I fought a guy named Ted. He was the biggest kid in our school, and I was one of the smallest. He was also really cool and really good at everything, so I naturally hated him. One day, I challenged him to a fight. He didn't want to fight me, but I wouldn't back down. He was backing away from me, and I kept pushing him down the hall like an annoying chihuahua. Finally, he took one swing and, before I knew it, I was on the ground, out cold. I couldn't believe it. I jumped back up for round two, and he knocked me down again. I was shocked. I thought, *How the heck is he doing this?*

I jumped back up again, and he knocked me out once again. When I sat up, my nose was bleeding, my mouth was bleeding, I was seeing stars, and wondering *What is he hitting me with?* It felt like some kind of force field. As I was getting up for round four, he put his foot on top of me and pleaded, "Man, just stop." So I grabbed his foot and bit it. He kicked me in the head to get me off, and then picked me up and helped clean me up.

I was mesmerized. Nobody had ever whipped my butt like that.

"Ted, how did you do that?" I asked.

"Well, I've been taking martial arts since I was two."

"Martial arts?"

"Yeah, it's where they teach you self-defense."

This was one of those life-changing moments. I knew I needed to learn this. Unfortunately, my parents disagreed.

"You already get into too many fights," my mom said. "Why would we pay for you to take lessons at it?"

I took it upon myself to find a karate dojo and began stealing money from my parents to take lessons. I practiced my katas in my room religiously until my mom found my gi, discovered what I'd been up to, and made me stop.

Without a positive outlet for fighting, I started fighting at school again. My parents were nearing the end of their rope with me. As a last-ditch effort, they put me in therapy. I *hated* that. I didn't want to talk. Plus, I was distracted by the fact that my therapist was missing part of his ear. He would try to ask me questions, and I'd ask him about his ear. I so badly wanted to know what had happened to it, but he would get irritated when I asked. He never did tell me. Throughout our sessions, I couldn't stop staring at it. He would catch me all the time and fuss at me to stop staring, but I couldn't help myself. It was the most fascinating thing I'd ever seen in my young life.

He finally asked me why I liked fighting so much. I told him that it was fun, and it just felt really good to punch things.

"Because you have anger issues?" he asked.

"I guess," I said. I was always angry.

"Have you ever trained?"

"Trained . . . to fight?"

"Yeah," he said.

I told him about my failed martial arts career, and at our next session, he surprised me with a punching bag.

"Whenever you feel angry and want to punch something," he said, "punch on this."

I drew pictures of the people who I felt had hurt me the most, pasted them on the bag, and went to town on it. I destroyed the bag before our next session.

"How did it go?" he asked. "Did it work?"

"Yeah!" I said, showing him the bag. "I can hit a lot harder and faster now."

I don't think that was the answer he was looking for. I'm pretty sure he thought I was psychotic and going to turn into an axe murderer.

When therapy failed to keep me out of trouble, my parents began looking to rehome me. I'm not sure how they went about it; I've always imagined them getting the church directory, starting with the A's, and just going down the list until they found another family who would take me in. That family turned out to be the Fieldings.

Living with the Fieldings was much better than being home—but they couldn't keep me forever, and after a few months, I ended up back at home. As soon as I returned, I was fighting and getting into trouble again.

A few months later, I went to live with the Franks. They had a son and daughter around my age, and they loved sailing. We would go sailing together on weekends. Their dad was really strict, which I respected. He was everything my dad was not, but after six months, they sent me right back to my family.

After the Franks, I guess my parents were too embarrassed to call the G families in the directory, so they got me out of their hair by passing me off to a family friend whom I'll refer to for the purposes of this story as "Dick."

Dick was the opposite of my straight-laced Catholic family; he was *always* high and seemed detached from reality, like he wouldn't care what trouble I might get into.

Boy, was I wrong! A week after I moved in, he treated me to a vegetarian casserole—his own creation—that looked like gruel and smelled disgusting. I moved it around on my plate, hoping to make it look like I'd eaten more than I had. But Dick was not so easily fooled, and screamed that he would beat the crap out of me if I didn't lick my plate clean. The crazed look in his eyes told me this was no empty threat. You better believe I ate every last bite of that revolting dish before he sent me to my room.

Shortly afterward, as I sat in my room feeling sick to my stomach, I heard him leave. I didn't know when or if he'd be back that night, and I was kind of relieved to be alone. When he finally did come home, I was asleep. He slammed the door open and flipped the lights on as he stormed into my room. I woke with my heart pounding. To my young eyes, he looked demon-possessed as he screamed at me nonsensically, accusing me of doing something I had never done. You know what I mean—trying to start a fight out of nothing, or trying to justify what he was about to do to me before it happened.

"What?" I asked, groggy from sleep, ready to poop myself from the adrenaline-fueled terror standing before me. I was completely confused. "What are you talking about?"

"You hit her! I know you hit her!" He must have screamed it a dozen times.

"I didn't hit anybody, Dick. I swear!"

Suddenly, he pulled me out of bed by my shirt and threw me across the room the way you only see in the movies. I flew through the air and landed in a heap. When I tried to scramble to my feet, he kicked me in the head, then pinned me to the floor and beat me until I was a bloody rag doll. The more I tried to get up, the more he'd beat me back down, until I finally realized that if I wanted to stay alive, I just had to stay there. I was convinced he was going to murder me that night.

I must have passed out. The next thing I remember was waking up, my body wracked with crippling pain, and having the strange feeling that I had been superglued to the floor. Everything was foggy, like a bad hangover. Every inch of my body hurt. I kept trying to sit up, but couldn't. I eventually realized the superglue keeping me stuck to the floor was a pool of my own dried blood.

I finally peeled myself free and crawled on all fours to the bathroom, where I pulled myself up to look in the mirror. I was horrified by what I saw staring back at me.

I didn't even look human. My nose was broken, both of my eyes were swollen, my lips were split wide open, and large pieces of skin were hanging like flaps from my black, blue, green, and purple face. All that went through my mind was that I had to get out of Dick's house as soon as humanly possible.

I showered and cleaned myself up as best I could. As I hobbled downstairs, every breath felt like a knife stabbing between my broken ribs. When I got to the living room, Dick was lying on the sofa, grinning at me.

"Look who finally decided to get up," he taunted. "You're a mess. You can't go to school looking like that. You're going to help me around the house today. Got it?"

I didn't dare say anything to contradict him. The only response he ever heard from me again was "Yes, sir."

"Good," he said with the emotional detachment of a sociopath. "I think we've settled things."

For two weeks, I was stuck at the house alone with Dick. He never beat me again, but I could not wait to make my escape. Until then, I played the perfect little soldier.

My first day back at school, I had to wear a hoodie to hide the remnants of my injuries. Everybody noticed that I wasn't pulling my hood down. My teacher finally demanded that I put it down, threatening detention if I didn't comply. When I reluctantly pulled it down and she saw what I was hiding, she sent me to the nurse's office. The nurse, highly concerned, asked what had happened. I told her I'd gotten into a fight. She must have seen right through my lie because she asked, "Mr. Kennedy, are you living in an unsafe environment?"

"No, ma'am. I'm perfectly safe." Another lie.

The last thing I wanted was someone coming to investigate. I just wanted to get the heck away from Dick. For the next few days, I'd pretend to leave for school, then break into nearby houses to steal enough money for a bus ticket back home.

When I arrived back at my parents' house and they saw me, they couldn't believe what had been done to me.

But I was still furious at them for sending me to live with him, and I vowed that if I ever saw Dick again, I was going to kill him. This was no idle kid's threat. I stole a gun and slept with it under my pillow, waiting for that day.

A few months later, I was at Ty's house when his mom got a call from mine.

"Joey," she said, "your mom wants you home. She said Dick is visiting."

She must have seen the evil glint in my eye, because she sent Ty running after me as I raced home. I flew into my house and ran to my bedroom to grab my .22.

Finding Dick at the top of the stairs, I pointed the gun at him and was about to pull the trigger, when Ty tackled me from behind, knocking me to the ground. The gun went off as it flew out of my hands.

My mom screamed, Dick screamed, and the police were called. I was cuffed and spent the night in the sheriff's office for accidentally discharging a weapon. Dick was terrified and left our house immediately. I never saw him again.

The next day, the sheriff dropped me off at a state-run group home. I didn't even get to pack a bag of clothes first. I would spend several months there before I was allowed to return home.

CHAPTER 4

UGLY TREE

There was a guy at the group home who would molest the girls at night. One time he tried to mess with me, but I had stolen a kitchen knife and made it clear that I was not afraid to use it. He didn't touch me or the girls in the house the rest of the time I was there, but when I told the adults what he had tried to do, they freaked out, and I was sent away soon after.

I was homeless for a while, couch-hopping between friends' houses, breaking into garages and cars, and even sleeping on the streets. One night, I broke into an old church to sleep. It was so creepy, I swear it was haunted. I heard weird noises the whole night. I never slept there again. Another night, I slept in a dumpster outside a downtown building that was being renovated. The dumpster was filled with cardboard boxes and old drywall, which kept it warm. There was an underground parking garage I also slept in several times even though it smelled like pee and was not nearly as warm as the dumpster.

In those days, I developed a sixth sense for survival. Ty's family tried to help me as much as they could, letting me stay in the trailer parked at the bottom of their driveway until my parents found out. When they learned I was at Ty's, they sent me to another group home that was more like a psychiatric ward, complete with a padded room where I once spent some time after smarting off to one of the counselors.

While I was at that group home, I heard the worst stories from some of the other kids in the joint about how their families had abused them. The stuff people do to young girls is just horrific. I wanted to kill anybody who would pick on someone just because they were smaller and weaker.

I forget how long I was at that group home. The next thing I remember is arriving back at my parents' house and finding it locked and dark. Unable to get in, I tried the next-door neighbors, who told me that my family had moved away!

In that instant, I flew into a blind rage. I had been shuffled from family to family, foster home to foster home, several group homes—and now I had been told that my family had simply abandoned me. Something inside my thirteen-year-old brain snapped. I broke into our house and began knocking pictures off the walls, breaking windows, tearing down curtains, flipping over furniture—I ransacked the place.

It turned out that my parents had not moved but had gone on an extended vacation to a second home I didn't even know they owned. At that moment, however, I was completely consumed by hatred and fury. I wanted to destroy everything in sight. My sense of abandonment erupted in unbridled rage. I finally collapsed in a heap, exhausted, screaming and cursing at God.

"WHY DOES NOBODY WANT ME? WHY DID YOU MAKE ME SO UNLOVEABLE! ARE YOU EVEN REAL?"

The police were called once again, probably by the same neighbor who misinformed me that my parents had moved. I spent the night at the sheriff's office before being sent to yet another group home until my parents returned. By the time they came back, they were at their wits' end. They had exhausted all their options with me. I hadn't given them much choice, but at that point, I was in no mood to make an effort with them. I was unapologetically angry.

I kept acting out in class and was expelled from six schools. The final expulsion came after I broke a kid's nose during a fight. His family threatened to sue both the school district and my parents. The school kicked me out, and my parents took out a second mortgage on the house to prep for legal fees. It was a stressful time.

Finally, my dad offered to take me on a camping trip, just the two of us. I should have known something was up. He never really interacted with any of us kids. When my older sister and I were younger, he tried to play with us, but he was pushing fifty, out of shape, and couldn't hang with us very long. As he and my mom started having their own kids, he retreated even further into his shell. But now were driving into the mountains, where we pitched tents and fished for a whole weekend. We talked while sitting under the stars by the campfire, and for the first time in my life, I felt like I had a real dad. We were bonding.

That's when the other shoe dropped.

When we got home, my mom was putting all my belongings on the front lawn. She had packed everything in garbage bags, like she was taking out the trash. I asked my dad what was going on, but he couldn't even look me in the face.

When my mom began tossing the bags into the trunk, I realized I was going on another trip. I kept asking what was going on until she finally explained that they were sending me away. Again.

I was furious. I'd just had a really nice weekend bonding with my dad, finally feeling like I belonged, and it was all just a ruse? My mom deflected by telling me I had brought it all on myself. Words were exchanged that wounded my soul for life.

I can't describe how consumed with anger I was over the next several hours as my dad drove deep into the mountains to the youth ranch that was about to become my new home. His awkward attempts at small talk didn't help, and after a little while he stopped trying. Sitting there in the silence, I loathed my parents for the way they had betrayed me. Sure, I was a bad kid, and I caused a lot of trouble, but this crossed every single line of trust.

We arrived at the ranch late that night. I got out of the car without a word to my dad as he drove away.

The ranch was a Christian-based boys' home, but it was run like a military camp. Everything was regimented. We rose at five, made our beds military-style, and showered. At breakfast, one of the "house dads" read a daily devotion from the Psalms or Proverbs. We had to eat everything on our plates. We could not leave *anything*, which was tough when it was liver and onions, stewed beets, or tomato juice from a can that had expired in 1947 (no joke).

A lot of our food came from the local mission or what grocery stores couldn't sell before the sell-by date. They would bring giant trucks to the boys' home, and we would sort out what was salvageable from what was moldy or rotting. We gave the spoiled food to the pigs and horses, and we ate everything else. It was the nastiest food you'd ever seen. It made Marine Corps food and MREs look gourmet, but they always made us take a serving of everything and clean our plates before we were allowed to leave the table. One kid actually puked on his plate, and they made him eat that and everything else until his plate was clean.

After breakfast, we had work details. Everybody had a different assignment, like barn duty, horse duty, irrigation duty, maintenance duty, and kitchen duty. The boys' home was also a fully functioning livestock and agricultural farm spread out over more than a hundred acres. We worked the fields and tended the pigs, cows, and chickens. We were responsible for moving all the pipes from field to field. We shoveled cow poop, cleaned out stalls, baled hay, harvested vegetables, and slaughtered animals. I don't know how we didn't die.

I was part of the irrigation crew, which was awesome because I got to play in industrial sprinklers every day in the 110-degree heat. Monday through Friday, we were bused down the mountain to town for school, returning to the ranch in the afternoons. The school kids picked on us "Ranch Boys." We never had any money, we smelled of farm animals, and we were either orphans or one step away from juvenile detention. We were the riff-raff at the high school, and everyone let us know it.

Discipline at the boys' home was doled out using a series of cards. Everybody started off with a white index card. You could earn stickers by doing chores and behaving well. After a certain number of stickers, you could trade your white index card for a colored card, which brought privileges like phone or TV time, outdoor time, and pizzas.

I never got a colored card. Instead, I got demerits. I was always doing extra work as punishment for fighting, mouthing off, and being a general menace to society.

Donovan, Dale, Ray, and Ms. Frederick ran the home. Donovan was a survivalist who always wore camo and took us on wilderness hikes to teach us about hunting, fishing, and living off the land. He would round us up, take us on a hike, then leave us in the wild for several days and wait for us to find our way home. I loved that. He was tough as nails, and I respected him.

Dale was a bear of a man. With his Burt Reynolds mustache, he looked like he was stuck in the 1970s. He was a severe disciplinarian, but we were bad freaking kids. This was our last stop before juvenile detention. We deserved every paddling we got.

Ray, on the other hand, was a small guy with a mischievous grin that made him look like he always knew something everyone else didn't. At meals, he ate what we ate, but he liked to pour it all into a bowl, mix it into a disgusting mush, and devour it with a maniacal grin as we gagged.

Ms. Frederick, one of the teachers, was the momma of the bunch. She was an absolute sweetheart, one of the kindest people I've ever met. She loved all of us unconditionally, no matter how bad we were. I still stay in touch with her.

When I was first sent to the boys' home, I was angry at God, angry at my parents, angry at everyone. My religious upbringing had resulted in a tumultuous relationship with God that left me unreceptive to what the boys' home was preaching, but Ray was relentless in trying to get me to "give God a try." We would debate for hours as I joined him for some punishing form of manual labor as a consequence for getting in trouble. He never crammed religion down my throat, but he always challenged my closed-mindedness on the subject. He found a way to reframe every excuse I came up with and turn it against me. It was infuriating, but it was also the first time I had been allowed to question everything without being judged or reprimanded. Ray was heroically longsuffering when it came to my never-ending questions.

After several months at the boys' home, God began to work on my heart. One moment changed everything.

The Reverend Hank Shoals, the retired minister who started the boys' home, was too old to keep up with a bunch of delinquent teenage boys, but he would visit from time to time. He wore a giant ring on his hand with which he loved to knock us boys upside the head. One day, when I was watching TV in the recreation room, he padded up behind me and smacked me with that ring.

"Kennedy, with me," he said.

I rubbed the side of my head, thinking, *What the heck was that for?* Reverend Shoals motioned for me to follow him outside to the porch, where he leaned against the railing, staring off into the distance.

"I hear you've been asking a lot of questions about God," he said matter-of-factly. He was always very matter-of-fact. "I'm gonna talk to you," he continued, not waiting for me to respond. "What do you see on that hill, Kennedy?"

Smart aleck that I was, I quipped, "Which hill?"

He knocked me upside the head again with his massive ring.

"All right, all right," I cried, squinting to inspect the horizon. I didn't see anything. Just a bunch of rocks. Maybe it was a trick question.

"I don't see anything, Rev," I answered.

"Look again," he instructed.

I squinted even harder, thinking maybe he saw an animal, but the more I looked, the more nothingness I saw. I mean, I was really looking. Finally, I responded, "I still don't see anything. Just a bunch of rocks and a tree."

"That's right. There's a tree," he nodded. "What do you think of the tree?"

This was one of the ugliest trees I had ever seen. It was gnarled and mangled and bare of leaves. It looked like it had weathered hell.

"It's ugly," I responded.

"Yeah, it's ugly," he declared. "It's a lot like you."

I stood there thinking, *Did this preacher just call me ugly?*

He must have known what I was thinking, because he popped me upside the head a third time with his obnoxious ring.

"Listen to me," he instructed. "That tree is the only living thing on that hillside. Nothing else has survived. Everything else has just died away, but its roots hold strong. It's weathered every single storm. Yeah, it's ugly and it's got the scars to prove it, but it's the toughest son of a gun up there. And that's you.

"Kennedy, you may have been dealt a bad hand," he went on, "but you have survived. You've got the lumps and bumps to prove it, but your roots go down deep and strong. God's gonna use that, son, if you'll let Him."

Then he walked off.

You could have knocked me over with a feather. I sat there for more than an hour looking at that tree on top of Eagle Rock, thinking, *Hmmm . . . maybe I should give God a try. What's the worst that could happen?*

CHAPTER 5

COINCIDENCE?

That tree opened my heart to the possibility of giving God a try. When I finally took that chance, I saw Him work in my messed-up teenage life in ways that I'm sure are no coincidence, even though I don't know what else to call them. The first coincidence came when I prayed with Ray.

"So what do I have to do to give God a try?" I asked.

"That's it. You just decided."

That sounded way too easy.

"You said you would give God a try, and you did," he stated.

The whole time I thought, *Yeah, right. There's no way God could love me. I'm a bad freaking kid*. I mean, I was the kid who broke into my parents' home and tore it apart. I had been stealing money from them since I was eight years old. I'd been kicked out of six different schools. There was no way God wanted anything to do with me, even if I was ready to give Him a shot.

"Kennedy," he told me, "God has got nothing but love for you, and He's got all the patience in the world. You just watch and see what He will do."

A few nights later, we were sitting in chapel. I had started trying to read the Bible. I absolutely hated reading—still do. But I was really trying to give God a try. I even started paying attention during the chapel readings. As I listened, I started thinking, *Okay, some of this stuff actually makes sense.* This night, Ray was talking about how lucky we were to live in a day where we had conveniences like electricity, heat, running water, and microwave ovens. "You know what?" he said. "God could take all of this away just like that!"

He snapped his fingers and, suddenly, all the lights went off.

We were all freaking out, going, "Okay, what kind of parlor trick is this?" We were looking around to see if one of the other guys was in on the trick. Reverend Shoals was there, and he just sat in his chair and started laughing. I was pretty sure that God hadn't just sent us back to the Dark Ages, but I was new to the whole God thing, so I couldn't be sure.

We didn't have electricity, heat, or running water to the home for two whole days. We eventually learned that someone had gotten into a car accident nearby and knocked down one of the powerlines. It just so happened that it was at exactly the moment when Ray snapped his fingers. Coincidence?

Shortly thereafter, I started having these conversations with God. It was never formal. Most of the time, I asked Him every question I could think of, and sometimes, it was like I could almost hear Him answering. One day I even heard Him ask me, "Kennedy, what do you want? I'm here for you. You have questions? Go ahead and challenge Me on them." Maybe I was going crazy, but I heard Him as clear as day. At first it kind of worried me that I was hearing this voice in my head, so I told Ray.

"Oh, that's just the Holy Spirit," he said.

I didn't know what a Holy Spirit was. I still don't. I thought maybe it was like a ghost or something, but Ray explained that the Holy Spirit was like the voice of God inside us. That sounded pretty cool, so I would question the Holy Spirit on everything that crossed my mind, and from time to time, He would answer back.

People would often bring roadkill to the boys' home for us to eat. Someone would hit a deer on the road, they'd bring it to us, and we'd skin it, cook it, and eat it. One day, I prayed, "God, I want to find a deer, and I want to find a bullet in its right shoulder." I have no idea why I prayed for that specific thing, but a few weeks later, Ray said that they had found a deer that had been shot about forty times. I went to help him see if there were any bullets left in the carcass before we ground it up. I reached my hand through its rib cage and started following all the bullet holes, looking for shrapnel. As I reached up through its right shoulder, I felt something cold and hard stuck in there. I pushed on it, and out of the right shoulder, a single bullet dropped. Even though the deer had been used as someone's target practice, that was the only bullet we found still in it. Coincidence?

Another time, we were up on the mountain pass. One of the things we often had to do at the boys' home was cut firewood. Of course, we couldn't just follow the road and cut whatever tree was right on the asphalt; we had to cut down the tree that was a mile off the road because they wanted to keep us busy so we would wear ourselves out. We'd spend all day walking half a mile out, cutting the tree down, and then hauling the logs back and forth to the truck waiting by the road for us. We had to fill the trucks up before we could return to the ranch.

It was the middle of winter up in the mountains, and it started snowing. Normally, that wasn't a big deal. We worked in the snow all the time. But this particular day, it snowed two feet in practically no time. By the time we realized we were in the middle of a blizzard, we were way up on the mountain. We hurried to load up the van, got in the vehicle, and started driving back, but the roads had iced over and the truck began to skid toward the cliff. In addition to the truck, we had twenty kids piled into an old passenger van. The truck's two front wheels went over the edge of the cliff; the undercarriage scraped against the ledge, which stopped it from skidding, and it got stuck. Our van also started sliding toward the edge. Donovan told us, "Boys, we're not gonna make it. Jump!"

My heart was pounding in my chest. I threw the door open and jumped out of the van. My buddy, who was right behind me, stood frozen in fear as the van kept sliding. None of the other kids could get out because he was blocking the exit. They started screaming and panicking. I don't know why I thought standing between the van and the ledge was a good idea—as if I could somehow stop it from going over—but in that moment, that's what I did. As the van slid toward me, all I could do in that moment was pray, "God, help them!" As soon as I said those words, the van miraculously came to a gentle stop right in front of me. The tire literally stopped against the big toe of my boot as I stood at the edge of the precipice. All the kids got out safely, and we pushed the van back to the middle of the road.

The blizzard was still going on, so we were stranded up on the mountain pass for several days, but we had plenty of firewood and plenty of gas. I almost blew my face off trying to light a fire. We had dug down into the snow as far as we could, thrown all the wood into a pile, soaked it in gasoline, and thrown matches on it. Unfortunately, the wood was soaking wet from all the snow. As I went to light a piece of bark, I saw the gas fumes rippling from underneath. The bark caught fire and there was a big *whoosh* as it flamed up. It singed my eyebrows, eyelashes, and my whole hairline. I quickly buried my face in the snow to get some relief from the flames. When I lifted my face out of the snowbank, everyone was cracking up, laughing at me. I looked so ridiculous—like Joe Pesci in *Home Alone*. Eventually we got a fire going and lived to tell about it. It took a while for my hair to grow back though.

During the summer, Donovan would take us on two-week survival hikes up into the mountains. All each of us could take with us was a wool blanket, a can of peaches, and a knife. That's it. For everything else, we had to live off the land. Donovan would teach us which plants we could and couldn't eat, how to trap and hunt small animals, and how to fish. Then it was up to us to survive.

On one particular hike, we were up in a big swampy area, and there were a lot of mosquitos. No matter where we tried to go, we could not escape the thick swarms. The buzzing was so loud, it would keep me up at night. After a few days of trying to outrun them, I finally found relief down by a lake that had a couple little islands in the middle. A few of the guys and I decided to swim out to them and spend the day swimming and fishing. I remember praying, "God, you've got to do something about these mosquitos, man. This is ridiculous."

When we made it to the islands, we saw a big puff of smoke coming toward us. At first, we thought it was one of the other kids playing with a campfire or something, but then more smoke started rolling in. Pretty soon, there was smoke everywhere. We started thinking, *Okay, this is getting weird. Something isn't right.* A few minutes later, a helicopter came flying over the mountain and we, being a bunch of stupid teenage boys, decided to flip the pilot off and moon him. We laughed as the helicopter flew over us, thinking we were such rebels, but then the lake started filling up with even more smoke. We decided to head back to our camp, and when we got there, we learned from one of our counselors that there was a wildfire on the mountain. We were trapped. To make matters worse, we realized that we had just shot the bird at our one potential rescue opportunity. Some of the guys started to freak out. I knew we were probably going to be safe unless we started seeing all the animals hightailing it for the lake. Animals' senses are much more heightened than ours, so as long as the animals didn't start running, we would be fine.

Sure enough, the animals started racing for the lake. We had to come up with a plan—and quick. A few of us decided to swim back out to the islands and wait for the smoke to blow over. Surely, surrounded by water, we would be safe. As we swam, I realized that all the mosquitos that had been plaguing us were gone. When I had asked God to give us a break from the mosquitos, a wildfire wasn't exactly what I had in mind, but it did the trick.

We spent that night on the island sleeping in a circle with our heads together and feet pointed outward. The smoke was so thick, I couldn't see more than a few feet ahead of me. We had covered our faces with our shirts and sleeping bags because we didn't want to breathe all of that smoke. We all laid there, praying, "God, You've got to save us! We don't want to die!" As I prayed, I saw a little flicker, and shouted, "Hey! I think I see something! Keep praying! Keep praying!" I realized that what I had seen was a star—the sky above us was almost clear. The fire went right around the lake and kept going. It burned over four hundred acres before it came under control. Just another coincidence, I'm sure.

After a year at the boys' home, I returned to my parents' and quickly fell back into my old habits of fighting and getting expelled. The school I was going to was so fed up with me that they sent me to an interim school where police officers would watch over you every second of the day. If you didn't show up for school or if you left early, they would arrest you and throw you into juvenile detention. I hated school, but I was such an idiot that I would just sit there and not do my work. So what happened? I got detention and had to stay late after school. I also had to do Saturday school because I was failing my classes. I ended up going to school six long days a week instead of the typical five. Then I had to go to summer school because I still couldn't get my grades up enough to pass my classes. For a kid who hated school, I ironically found ways to spend way more time there than I could have.

By the time I was a senior, my GPA was 0.33, and I needed a 0.4 to graduate. I had already enrolled in the National Guard and could not take my Marine oath of enlistment until I got my high school diploma. Even though I had backslid in my faith since leaving the boys' home, I prayed, begging God to help me graduate.

Miraculously, I graduated from Bremerton High School in 1988 with a 0.4 GPA. I still don't know if my Marine recruiter pulled some strings to help me get that, or if my teachers were just so sick of seeing my face in their classes that they fudged a few numbers to get me out, but I graduated high school and went straight into the Marine Corps.

My senior year, I was not hanging out with the best crowd. My friends and I would routinely commit felonies for fun. I knew that if I stayed in Bremerton, I would end up in prison or dead, so I saw the Marine Corps as my way to a better life. The week I left for boot-camp, my two best friends decided to go to the marina and steal a boat. They took a paddleboat out with a ladder and found a boat they thought was empty. When the first guy reached the top and swung his leg over to board the boat, he found an old man waiting for him with a rifle.

"Wrong boat, punk," he said before pulling the trigger. The bullet went straight through my friend's head, killing him, and hitting my other friend, who was right behind him, in the ankle. He fell overboard but lived to tell about it.

My other friend was buried, but because I was away at boot camp, I didn't get to attend the funeral. Had I not already been there, I know

I would have gone with them and insisted on being the first man up that ladder. God spared me certain death that day.

Again, I'm sure it was just a coincidence.

CHAPTER 6

THE FEW, THE PROUD

Ever since I was a kid, I had wanted to join the Marines. My Uncle Dan was a Marine, and he was the toughest guy I'd ever met. He was a giant of a man with a big, booming voice. As a rambunctious kid, I was always running around making noise and, after a while, I must have been annoying the heck out of him because he turned around and bellowed, "HEY. STOP THAT. BE QUIET." Scared the living crap out of me.

From that moment on, I was in awe. He just commanded respect in the way he carried himself, and I wanted to be just like him. He was the only adult who never treated me like a little kid. He didn't have any kids of his own—in fact, he didn't really like kids—but he would let me watch John Wayne and old war movies with him which was cool. We never really talked, but when he told me that he had been a Marine just like the guys in the movies, fighting for our country, that was all I wanted—the patriotism, the manliness, the physical combat, seeing them fight the enemy, and wearing those dress blues. It was the epitome of everything I wasn't. I was a punk who had zero discipline. I knew joining the Marines was the only way I could ever hope to make something of myself.

At my bootcamp graduation ceremony, Uncle Dan came down and handed me a little box. When I opened it, inside was his Marine Corps ring from 1951, when he fought in Korea. He had always worn it when I was a kid, and now he was giving it to me. It was the first thing that anyone had ever seen fit to pass down to me. Years later, when my son, Jacob, graduated from Marine bootcamp, I passed that same ring down to him. Before Uncle Dan died, Jacob and I went to visit him, and we sat there, three generations of Marines, all together. It was one of the proudest moments of my life.

I love the Marines. It's not like being in the Army or the Navy. Marines are what we've become. It's who we are for life. To this day, when I hear the oath of enlistment, it makes the hairs on the back of my neck stand up with pride. I took that oath with the utmost seriousness because I had never belonged to or really believed in anything before. Nothing had ever meant that much to me. Being a Marine wasn't something given to me, and it wasn't something I stole—I had to earn it with blood, sweat, and tears.

Bootcamp is designed to break you down physically and mentally, expose your weaknesses, and then build you back stronger. Tougher. Everybody west of the Mississippi River goes to San Diego for bootcamp. As soon as we got off the airplane, it started. The new recruits were met at the airport by some of the meanest-looking dudes I'd ever seen. Everyone was looking around, totally lost, when one of the drill instructors immediately began barking at everyone to get on the bus. As soon as we did, they screamed at us to put our heads between our knees and not even dare to look out the window to see where we were going. They then drove around with us like that for what seemed like several hours, screaming at us the entire time. Mind you, base is right by the airport. That was all a mental game designed to discombobulate everyone and start breaking us down, making us feel lower than scum.

When the bus finally arrived at base, another equally tough-looking Marine got on it. This guy was even bigger than the first guy, if you can believe it. He took up the entire doorway and began yelling, "YOU HAVE THIRTY SECONDS TO GET OFF THIS BUS STARTING NOW!" He was blocking the whole doorway, not about to move, so we started opening emergency exits and windows trying to get the heck off the bus.

Once we were finally out, the drill sergeant screamed at us to stand on some yellow footprints painted on the ground. As we formed ranks, it seemed like twenty more drill instructors started crawling out of the woodwork to berate us. It was absolutely terrifying. If we made the mistake of looking one of them in the eye, he would scream, "WHO TOLD YOU THAT YOU COULD LOOK AT ME! DON'T YOU EFFING LOOK AT ME!" No matter what any of us tried to do, it was wrong.

They finally sent us to processing and shaved our heads with a buzzer that seemed to grind against our scalps. Worst haircut of my life. We received our uniforms, and they showed us to the crappiest barracks you can imagine. The whole time, I was wondering if I had just made the biggest mistake of my life. We went from being scared to absolutely petrified. By the time we finally went to sleep that night, we were all emotionally and physically exhausted.

It seemed like I had just closed my eyes when the most horrendous noise woke me up. The drill instructors were throwing fifty-gallon metal garbage cans down the aisle of our barracks. The metal clanging of the trash cans on the linoleum floors echoed off all the hard surfaces. We all jumped out of bed to await inspection in our skivvies. They scrutinized us from head to toe, looking for any imperfection as an excuse to make us do pushups. By the time we all showered and hit the mess hall, our cafeteria food looked like gourmet food—especially compared to what I had eaten at the boys' home. As we went down the line, we had to do a fancy sidestep, stick our arms out with stick-straight precision, wait for the servers to scoop whatever mush they were serving onto our plates, and then fancy-sidestep to the next station.

My drill instructor was a short, mean Mexican named Sergeant Salazar. He wore little clickers on his boots and a wide, stiff-brimmed hat that, when he marched up to one of us and got in our face, would cut us on the nose or mouth. He introduced himself to our unit with a twisted grin.

"I am your mother," Salazar said. "I am your everything. If you make *me* mad, there is nobody to save you."

Bootcamp was divided into three phases. Phase One was by far the worst, mentally and physically. It was designed to separate the men from the boys. We learned everything about what made Marines the most elite fighting force in the world. Phase One taught us all about Marine Corps customs and courtesies. We learned how to march, we studied all the battles, weaponry, and weapons systems. We learned about the history of the Marines—all the famous battles and heroes of the Corps. The drill instructors would test us on anything and everything we were taught at any moment. If we didn't answer correctly, they would thrash us.

Phase Two was not as hard as Phase One, but it was still hard. In Phase Two, we were sent to Camp Pendleton. We spent two weeks living in the field as they taught us how to survive long periods without food and water. We had field training, mock wars, tactical training, rifle training, and hump training, where we would go on long hikes in full combat gear. We also had to learn to swim in full combat gear. They would put us through drills in the pool where we would have to save one of our instructors from drowning. Once we got to him, he would sink to the bottom of the pool like a deadweight, and we would have to use all our strength and skill as swimmers to pull him back to the top. Once we got him to the top, he would start fighting us. We would have to struggle against his flailing and screaming to make him submit, and then swim to the side of the pool. It was one of the most physically challenging things I had endured, and I was one of the best swimmers in the group. By the time I got the instructor into a submissive state, I was seeing stars, my heart felt like it was about to explode inside my chest. I had inhaled a gallon of water, and I thought I was going to die. No sooner did I make it to the side of the pool than one of the educators entered with a tourist group and made me do the entire drill over again to show off for them. I had pneumonia for over a week after that.

Phase Three was where the whole package came together. We had swim qualification, lots of marching and inspections, and we had to spit-polish everything in preparation for our final drills. At the end of those thirteen weeks, we had all earned the right to be called Marines. Graduating from boot camp was and still is one of the proudest achievements of my life.

After that, I went to Camp Johnson in North Carolina. I got selected for motor transport to be a mechanic, so I went to school to learn all about the vehicles that the Marine Corps uses. After my time there, I was sent to Camp Hansen in Okinawa, Japan, where I lived in absolute sin and debauchery. There was no drinking age there. Right outside the base was a little town with nothing but bars, whorehouses, and souvenir shops where you could buy cheap crap to send back home. Every night, I would go out with the other guys and get drunk off my butt. Marines being Marines, we loved to fight. When there was no enemy to fight, we would get drunk and fight each other. I broke my nose so many times in those fights that it is now permanently crooked. Later I would have to get a nose job to try to undo some of the damage.

One night, I got especially plastered. I woke up the next morning and didn't have a clue where I was. As I opened my eyes and tried to remember what had happened, I realized it was raining, and I was outside. On a roof. In my underwear. Suddenly, I became aware of some commotion coming from below and looked over the side of the roof to see a little Japanese lady standing on the ground, waving a pitchfork and screaming at my buddy, who had just fallen off the roof. She was screaming at him in Japanese (neither of us spoke Japanese) and prodding him with her pitchfork.

In that moment, I realized I needed to start doing some things differently, so I began working out like a fiend, eating 100 percent healthy food, and studying martial arts. (I used to look good before I had to go through a lawsuit. Since then, I've aged like a president.)

I got my black belt and then began teaching martial arts to some of the other guys. I got really good at fighting. Maybe a little too good. During my time in Japan, I got sent to Korea for a joint operation, and I got in a little trouble. I was a young lance corporal, two years into the Marines at that point, and I was assigned to the unit that guarded the headquarters. One night after our unit had gone to sleep, the non-commissioned officers got a bit drunk. They came in and were being loud and obnoxious, waking everybody up, but none of us could do anything because they were NCOs. They outranked us. But one of the guys thought he could deal out a little payback the next morning. His job was to wake everybody up, so he came into the tent yelling like we were back in bootcamp. He went over to one of the corporals and started yelling in his face, "Corporal! Corporal, get up!"

The corporal was still pretty drunk and combative. He got up and began pushing the other guy around. "Who do you think you're freaking talking to!"

On that day, that kid was on guard duty, which meant that he outranked everybody. People do not challenge the person on guard duty—so that day, he even outranked the corporal, though he was only a private first class. He would have been nervous to stand up to the corporal unless he knew we had his back.

"Corporal, lay off him," I said.

The corporal rounded on me angrily, and yelled, "Kennedy, shut the F up!"

Then he went back to knocking the PFC around. The PFC looked over at me and asked, "Kennedy, can I hit him back?"

"Knock him out," I replied.

This made the corporal even angrier. "Kennedy! I told you to shut the F up. Stay out of this!"

I was fed up with the way the corporal was acting, so I got up.

"You do not talk to me like that," I commanded.

He came at me and took a swing, and something in me snapped like it did the day I thought my parents had moved away without telling me. I started beating the crap out of him. I was holding his head down on the ground and just laying into him. My fists were flying.

One of the other guards started to get nervous and pulled me off of the corporal, who was lying on the ground holding his head and groaning in pain. I slowly calmed down from my blind rage and took in the situation. When I saw what I had done, I went, "Oh my God."

The PFC looked at me and said, "Kennedy, you need to get out of here."

I grabbed my stuff and went to start my shift on guard duty. The whole time, I was totally paranoid. A little while later, one of my guys came up. "Kennedy, we need you to come back to the tent," he said.

"What's up?" I asked nervously.

"Corporal is messed up bad. He's asking for you."

Now I was really nervous. "Are you serious?"

"Yeah. He won't let anybody touch him. He's asking only for you."

"Crap."

I headed back to the NCO tent and peeked in to see how much trouble I was in. I was convinced the corporal had a shovel, ready to ambush me and knock me out cold. Instead, he was sitting on the rack with his whole head wrapped in a blood-soaked towel.

"Is that Kennedy?" he asked.

"Yeah?" I piped up, my voice breaking like a prepubescent teenager's.

"Come in here, man," he said. "Look, I'm not gonna do anything to you, but you've got to fix me up."

I walked over to him tentatively. "Are you okay?"

"I don't know, man. I don't feel good."

"Let me see," I offered as he unwrapped his head.

I was appalled by what I saw. His bottom lip was split all the way down to his chin, and his top lip was split all the way up to his nose. His nose was split on both sides, just hanging off his face like a flap. Blood was pouring from him. It looked like something out of a horror movie.

"Corporal, you're pretty messed up," I told him. "I can't fix this. We're gonna have to call Doc."

"No, no, Kennedy. Just fix me up."

"I'm telling you, I *can't*. You are jacked up."

I could see the bone where his upper and lower lip had split. I was thinking he could die. I called the doc and they ended up medevacking him out of there. That's how bad it was.

The MPs read me my rights, and I had to see a lawyer. I asked to request mast to the commanding general, which would allow me to directly communicate my grievance to my CO for his consideration.

If that didn't settle things, I wanted a court martial. They told me they would get back to me. Whenever someone requests a court martial, they have to take it seriously and do a formal investigation. The lawyer told me, "You're going to have to take a Page Eleven for assault. You might get demoted or confined to the barracks."

A Page Eleven was the lowest form of nonjudicial punishment. It meant a mark on your permanent record that would follow you forever. If you had a Page Eleven and wanted to reenlist, nobody would take you. Your military career was done. I did *not* want a Page Eleven on my record. (Later on in my career, I would end up getting several, but these were the days before everything became computerized. When I got a Page Eleven, I would call up my buddy who worked in admin and get him to remove it from my hard-copy record.)

"Whoa, whoa, whoa," I objected. "He hit me first."

"That's irrelevant," the attorney stated. "He's an NCO."

"No, it's not irrelevant," I argued. "Self-defense is still a valid defense."

"Well, aren't you Mr. Lawyer," he smarted off.

"I know my rights," I told him. (I didn't know my rights.) "I'll go before the court martial because this is bull. I've got thirty guys who witnessed it. The guy was drunk and took a swing at me, and I reacted in self-defense."

He looked at me like I was a Class A pain in his rear. "If you think you can defend yourself, go for it."

After some time, the staff sergeant came over to me. "Kennedy, we're not going to press charges because it was self-defense. The only thing I want to know is what you hit him with."

"My fists," I answered.

"Come on, son," he pressed. "Not with that kind of damage. Did you have a night stick or a flashlight?"

"No, sir. I didn't have a weapon."

"Come on, Kennedy."

"There were thirty other guys in there. Ask any of them. I did not have a weapon."

The staff sergeant was shocked that I had done that much damage with my bare hands. From that moment on, I vowed never to snap like that again. I stuck to controlled fighting environments like wrestling, boxing, combat training, and martial arts. I never used my fists to settle a score like that again.

CHAPTER 7

DESERT STORM

Every Marine dreams of combat. It's what we train so intensely for. In early 1991, when my unit got the call that we were deploying to Kuwait for Operations Desert Shield and Desert Storm,[1] I was ecstatic. We were going to war!

We packed all our combat gear, our weapons and ammunition, I kissed my then-wife, Amy, goodbye (I got married shortly before the war broke out—more on that in the next chapter), and headed to the airport. I was riding high on the adrenaline of deployment as we waited to board our flight. After waiting at the airport for several hours, we got the order to stand down. Our flight had been canceled. We would try again the next day.

This went on for three or four days in a row. We'd show up to the airport, packed and ready to deploy, then we'd get the call that our

---

1 Desert Shield was what the operation was called before the war officially started. We were in Saudi Arabia and Kuwait for seven months with Desert Shield before the war began. The war itself was called Operation Desert Storm, which only lasted about seven to ten days.

plane was canceled. We'd take all our gear home and arrive in time for dinner. It had become a running joke that I'd kiss my wife goodbye as I headed overseas in the morning and ask her where she wanted to go for dinner that night when I inevitably got the order to stand down.

The last day we showed up to the airport, I was already thinking about that night's dinner plans when we all of a sudden got the go order. It was for real this time. We were going to board the aircraft and ship off. The adrenaline kicked in as we loaded up the plane with all our gear. This was before cell phones, so I didn't get to even let my wife know that we had finally gotten our marching orders. I just simply didn't go home for dinner that night—or for seven months after.

Because all the fighter jets and cargo planes had already deployed to Kuwait, we loaded our gear onto a commercial plane. We had grenades, light antitank rockets, and live ammunition in our rifles, and we were dressed in full combat gear with our flak jackets and helmets. When we landed, we were ready to set up a perimeter and start shooting people.

As we waited to take off, I noticed a flight attendant was looking anxious.

"Ma'am," I said bravely, "we're fully trained for this. You're going to be safe."

"Oh, that's not what I'm worried about," she answered. She paused nervously, then lowered her voice so as not to alarm everyone. "We've never been this heavy before."

Now, I was no pilot, but the way she said that did not sound good. A few minutes later, the captain got on the loudspeaker and said, "I just want to let you know, you guys pack well for war. I'm gonna do my best to get this aircraft off the ground, but we might not be able to make it."

Up to that point, I had been too filled with the excitement of finally being deployed to remember that I had an intense fear of flying. That quickly changed. Here I was, Mr. Tough Guy Marine, trying not to let on how scared I was. I sat back in my seat and watched as the flight attendant cinched up her seatbelt, a worried frown on her face. I was thinking, *Oh, this isn't good.*

You know how when an airplane goes full-throttle and the pilot releases the brakes, it pushes you back in your seat? As we heard the engines on this flight go full throttle, nothing happened. After a few moments, we barely started inching forward. By the time we started to pick up a little speed, I could see the end of the runway up ahead. The flight attendant was white-knuckling the grip on her armrest, and I was about to start hyperventilating. I pictured the captain in the cockpit pulling back on the yoke as hard as he could, grinding his teeth and praying the plane cleared the fence at the end of the runway.

By some miracle, we got the aircraft up into the air but, when we landed to refuel in Germany, we came down so hard, we broke the landing gear. It snapped under the excessive weight of our combat gear. We were stuck on the tarmac forever because the airline had to call in emergency crews to fix the landing gear. We could not simply change planes, because no one else was flying into the war zone. We had to wait in the pouring rain outside for hours as they fixed the landing gear, and then the insanely slow takeoff scenario repeated itself as we took off for our base in Saudi Arabia.

By the time we landed in Saudi Arabia, our NCOs were briefing us about how to set up the perimeter. As soon as we touched down, we stormed out of the plane, weapons loaded and ready for combat. We were expecting to come under heavy fire immediately. To our surprise, not only was there no combat, but there were a lot of guys walking around in T-shirts, looking at us as if we were crazy. *Where's the war?* I thought as I looked around. I didn't realize we would have to move all of our gear to the warzone several hundred miles away.

Saudi Arabia was 112 degrees Fahrenheit around the clock, with absolutely horrible humidity. The air was so saturated that even the buildings seemed to sweat. I don't think our clothes ever dried in the seven months we were there.

During that time, we got really close as a unit. We spent a lot of time thinking of the dumbest things to do. Once a week, we would get to shower outdoors under these giant water valves. We were all naked, trying to cool off and wash the endless dust and sand from our bodies, when some camels came around. I had the bright idea to try to lasso a camel. We piled into one of our military vehicles (still buck naked, mind you) and fashioned some ropes into a lasso. We took turns trying to lasso the camels from the back of a truck as they were running away. I was adamant that I was going to catch one if it was the last thing I did. I yelled at my buddy driving the truck to get closer. He got so close that he actually bumped right into a camel, which was so startled that I was able to get the lasso over his head. The camel freaked out, took a hard right away from the vehicle, and ripped me out of the truck along with him. He took off running full speed; he had to have been going twenty-five miles an hour, dragging my naked butt across the desert sands behind him. My buddies were laughing at me as I hung on for dear life, getting sand burns everywhere.

Another time, we had made camp and dug out a giant trash dump the size of a football field to throw all our waste into. Before we moved on, we would burn the trash so as not to leave anything useful for our enemy. This particular day, the thirty-thousand-gallon fuel truck had just been refilled, so my buddies and I decided to unload the whole thing on this trash dump and watch it burn. When we lit it, it exploded into giant flames. It was really cool, except that the fire kept getting bigger and bigger and bigger. There was no sign of it dying down. Thick black smoke billowed up into the clear skies. We began to realize that this wasn't good. We were drawing a lot of attention to ourselves.

Pretty soon, we started getting radio calls from officers screaming at us, "WHAT ON EARTH ARE YOU IDIOTS DOING! WE CAN SEE YOU ON SATELLITE! YOU JUST GAVE AWAY OUR EFFING POSITION!"

We got in so much trouble for that. The staff NCOs called us over and said, "Since you boys seem to like to burn stuff so much, you're gonna be on excrement duty from now on."

Excrement duty is exactly what it sounds like: You burn human feces. To say it stinks is the understatement of the century. It got old really fast, so my buddy, Freddie and I started looking for ways to make it more entertaining. We found some hollow poles we used to set up our netting so aerials couldn't see us, and we would poke them into the fifty-five-gallon drums we would remove from under the outhouse seats. When we poured diesel into the drums and lit them on fire, we would pack the hollow poles with poop and fling the flaming excrement at each other.

Because we were in the middle of the desert without indoor plumbing, we would build outhouses on the edge of our camp. We kept some very "educational" reading material in there to keep our minds active.[2] I was out there late one night engrossed in a *Wall Street Journal* article[3] when I started to feel like somebody was watching me. It was pitch black, and I had nothing but a flashlight on me. I didn't even have my rifle. I shined my light out the little window and saw a giant camel head right next to mine. It was like he was trying

2 Okay, it was *Playboy*. But we read it for the articles, I promise!
3 OKAY, it was *Playboy*! Geez.

to read the magazine right over my shoulder. I fell off the outhouse commode, screaming. The camel startled at my reaction and hit its head on the top of the window opening. I chased it away with my drawers still down around my ankles. Camels, it turns out, are incredibly silent when they walk.

We moved across Saudi Arabia to the Kuwait border in convoys of thousands of vehicles—vehicles as far as the eye could see. I was with Task Force Ripper, one of the largest task forces ever formed, as part of the wrecker jump team. Whenever one of the vehicles broke down, my buddy Earl and I would leave the convoy, bring our wrecker out to tow the truck back to safety, and do whatever we needed to do to fix it.

One night, as we were driving, one of the ammo trucks broke down. I was going to drive it behind the wrecker to try to get it back to our camp, but as soon as I tried to start the engine, it flat-out died on us.

At night, the desert is pitch black—darkness like you can't even imagine. We couldn't see our hands in front of our faces. We couldn't use our vehicle headlights because we didn't want to give our position away to the enemy, so we relied on tactical lights. Tactical lights are two or three little red dots on the back of each vehicle that are used in blackout conditions. They're really difficult to see in good conditions, let alone the endless dust and sand of the desert. This night after we broke down, the lead vehicle took off without us, leaving us in the middle of a minefield. Engineers had done their best to clear a path for us in advance. By "clearing a path," I mean that they put up wooden markers with rope outlining where they had swept a clear path for us to drive on.

The path was very narrow, just barely accommodating our wide military vehicles. We could see mines everywhere just beyond the ropes; if we veered off the path just a hair, we could hit one.

Once we fixed the ammo truck and were back on the path trying to catch up to the rest of the vehicles, I started messing with Earl. Earl was very tightly wound and easily excitable. I would say, "Hey, Earl, you think they cleaned all the mines out? Maybe there's deeper ones waiting for the tanks. We're hauling all this extra weight; I hope we don't set one off."

He was already freaked out, so he began cursing at me. "Shut the F up, Kennedy! That's not funny!"

"Make sure you stay between the lines, Earl. Don't veer off the path, Earl." I kept messing with him the whole way back to the rest of our convoy. Meanwhile, Earl had a death grip on the steering wheel, totally focused on trying to follow the tactical lights in blackout conditions. I kept reaching under the steering wheel and grabbing it just to mess with him. He cursed me out the whole drive back.

When we breached the two minefields on the Saudi Arabia/ Kuwait border, the skies began to turn black and we started seeing flames. The Iraqis had bombed the oil fields, which seemed to light the sky on fire. The ground vibrated like a continuous earthquake from the power of them. Imagine the sound of fighter jet engines on full throttle multiplied by a thousand. The flames were so powerful and hot, it felt like they would melt the flesh off your bones. Even during the day, the skies were so dark from the smoke that it felt like nighttime. I had never experienced anything like it before, nor have I experienced anything like it since. It was as if we were journeying through Hell.

In addition to the heat of the desert and the smoke from the burning oil fields, there was also the danger of gas attacks. We had to wear gas masks all the time because the Iraqis would use frog missiles that would pump out gas. One night, a missile landed just outside our fighting holes. Whenever we stopped for the night, we would dig fighting holes to sleep in and take turns keeping watch. We thought this missile must have been a dud because nothing happened for a few minutes. Some buddies and I went out to inspect it, when suddenly, the thing exploded and started pumping out smoke and gas. We freaked out, hurrying to put our gas masks on and radio all the other troops in the vicinity. We spent the rest of that night at 100 percent alert for potential nuclear, biological, and chemical attacks, wearing charcoal-filled hazmat suits with thick, heavy boots, gloves, and gas masks (known as Mission-Oriented Protective Posture [MOPP] Level 4) in the unbearable desert heat.

Later that night, we got called out to tow an ammo trailer that had broken down. As we brought it back to camp, Earl was backing up the truck, and another guy and I were holding up the massive, hundred-pound tailgate so I could hook it into place. As I did, the ammo trailer started rolling away. The buddy who was helping me panicked and ran off after it—dropping the tailgate right on my head, smashing it between the tailgate and the bumper. It felt like one of those moments in a cartoon when the character's eyes pop a full foot out of its head. I fell to the ground, dazed and confused.

My buddy ran back over, asking if I was okay. I couldn't stand up. Each time I tried to get my legs under me, I would fall back down on my butt. When I tried to brace myself and walk a few steps, I'd face-plant into the sand. My buddy was worried and called the doc to come take a look at me. It didn't take long to figure out I had a pretty severe concussion. They wouldn't let me work on the truck anymore—I was so sick, I didn't even want to—so they told me to go back to my fighting hole. I spent the rest of the night there, throwing up from the concussion. I couldn't see or think straight. I knew that if anyone fell into my hole, it would be futile to try to shoot, so I asked for some grenades as protection.

I was so out of it that I climbed out of the fighting hole at one point and started trying to juggle the grenades for Earl's amusement.

He didn't think it was so funny. As he was chewing me out, his face all of a sudden lit up in this white light. Before I knew it, I was blown into the fighting hole, and I landed right on top of Earl. We were far enough away from the rocket not to have any limbs blown off, but we were still close enough to be within the blast radius. It knocked me out cold for a few minutes. When I woke up, I thought for sure I had died.

As I slowly realized that I was still alive, covered in sand and dust, I felt someone patting me down frantically. I saw Earl underneath me and realized he was feeling me up. I was thinking, *Dude, what the heck?,* and I started fighting him off, accusing him of being a perv, when he yelled, "Kennedy, you idiot, we just got blown up! I'm trying to see if you're okay!" It dawned on me that he was patting me down to make sure I still had all my limbs and wasn't on fire or bleeding.

Thankfully, I was still in one piece. I was so happy (and still completely concussed) that I jumped up and started screaming, "WOOHOO! THAT WAS BETTER THAN SPLASH MOUNTAIN AT DISNEYLAND!" Earl quickly yanked me back into the fighting hole. "Shut up, you effing idiot!"

For months, we would move, dig our fighting holes, shoot, repeat. Move, dig, shoot, repeat. It was like that all day, every day. After a while, we got tired. The adrenaline had worn off. We were getting close to the Al Mubarak Airfield in Kuwait, and it was getting dark early because of the smoke. When night fell, between the blackness of night and the thick smoke from the oil fields, we couldn't see our own hands in front of our faces. There were no night vision goggles to be had. Our guns were worthless because you have to be able to see to shoot. Our master sergeant came to check on us and told me and Earl that if anybody fell into our fighting hole that night, we were to stab the crap out of them with our KA-BAR fighting knives, or pull a grenade and blow everybody up.

We sat there in the dark for hours on alert. Most fighting holes contained four men so that two could sleep while two remained awake on watch. Earl and I were the only two people in our fighting hole in full MOPP 4 gear, so we both had to stay awake all night. We sat in the dark, straining our ears for every little sound, but against the fire and rumble of the burning oil fields, we couldn't hear anything meaningful. The MOPP gear further inhibited our senses, muffling sounds, limiting our already restricted vision even further, and making it difficult to move with the thick gloves and pads. Our eyes began playing tricks on us in the dark—we would think we'd see a little bit of light or something moving. That added to the paranoia.

In the middle of the night, our squawk box radio went off. I responded, "Kennedy position four, what's going on?"

The voice on the other end replied, "Iraqis in the POS, I repeat, Iraqis in the POS."

That meant that someone had spotted Iraqi insurgents in our position. I could feel Earl tense up beside me as our adrenaline kicked back in.

"Tell me you're BS-ing me," I said with all the fierceness I could muster in my voice.

"Negative."

"What degree?" I asked.

"Northwest."

I heard Earl whisper to me, "Kennedy, we're in the northwest sector."

Crap.

"Inside the perimeter or outside?" I radioed back.

"Cannot confirm. All we know is there are Iraqis in the northwest sector of the POS."

"You better be lying to me," I warned. We joked all the time about seeing Iraqis to psych each other out. I prayed this was another instance of our command post pulling our legs.

"I'm not lying this time. Good luck. CP out."

The radio fell silent. We were without night vision goggles or the use of our rifles. We were in full MOPP 4 gear in the pitch blackness. Imagine being in a sensory deprivation chamber in the middle of a war zone. That's what it felt like. Without the ability to see or even hear, every moment felt unbearably tense. The sound of my heartbeat echoed in my ears. Every breath seemed dangerously loud. I prayed nobody would fall into our fighting hole. Throughout the night, I thought for sure I could hear people walking through the sand around us, but I couldn't tell for sure.

We were straining for every bit of sound above the roar of the burning oil fields to give us some kind of intel in the pitch blackness when suddenly, our hole caved in a little bit and we heard a loud *HEE HAW!*

No joke, a donkey had almost fallen into our hole. It scared the literal crap out of Earl. (I might have peed a little.) I was about to pull my grenade and blow us all up over a literal dumb ass! We were so tightly wound that night.

But the adrenaline can't last forever. Eventually, when it wears off, you crash. Earl and I were doing "touch-and-go's" where you nod off and then jerk back awake in a frustrating cycle of sleeplessness. I was rubbing my face trying to stay awake when out of nowhere, a bright light flashed and I heard a gunshot go off. I felt a bullet whiz past my face and, for a split second, I thought for sure I was dead.

"Earl, somebody's shooting at us!"

He jolted upright. "Where did it come from?"

"I think it was right outside the hole."

We fruitlessly tried to look around us. "I can't see anything."

"Neither can I."

"It was from right over here. It just flew past my head!" I futilely pointed toward where the flash had gone off, and my hand touched where Earl was sitting.

"Earl?" I asked.

"Yeah, Kennedy?"

"How's your rifle?"

We had a habit of sleeping with our rifles in our hands ready to shoot.

"I didn't shoot you, man," he answered defensively.

"Is your dust cap on?" I asked.

I heard Earl swear under his breath. "No. Do you think anybody else heard it?"

"Earl!"

"Dude, I'm sorry!"

Meanwhile, people from the neighboring holes started calling out, "Who's shooting?" "Did you hear shots fired?"

Earl whispered to me, "We can't tell them it came from us!"

It had been an accidental discharge that almost blew half my face off. I was so mad at Earl the rest of the night.

When the sun finally came up the next morning, we saw hoofprints from the donkey that had almost fallen into our fighting hole. Next to them were boot prints weaving throughout all of our fighting holes. The Iraqis had been in our quadrant, and they had used donkeys and goats to help them navigate around our holes. They had been all around us, and the shuffling noises in the sands we thought we heard *had* actually been insurgents. Seeing how close they had gotten to us was sobering. They were right outside our hole and walking through our position the whole night. That was the first time it really hit me that we could have died, especially if the enemy had had night vision goggles when we were totally blind. Thank God, they didn't.

Being at war is a strange experience. You are either in a state of adrenaline overdrive or burnout. There is no real in between. You constantly expect an attack. You are asked to sacrifice yourself if you come into contact with enemy soldiers rather than risk giving them any useful intel or tools to use against your fellow Marines. You're also surrounded by senseless death. You have been trained to dehumanize your enemy so you can effectively kill him without a second thought, but you are also faced with the death of your brothers. You become like a robot, removed from human emotions.

It makes you wonder about the afterlife. It definitely challenged my faith. I wondered how a God who was supposed to be all-loving could allow the carnage of war. I had seen buddies get shot, lose limbs, have their brains ooze out the back of their heads, go into shock, and die on the battlefield.

I worked with the wounded a lot. We would pick those guys up and take them to the medical tents. The docs would assess them based on chance of survival. You would think that the worse off you are, the quicker you would get in to see the doc, but it was not like that. If you had gotten your arm blown off and were bleeding out, you were put in the Expectancy Pile. Nobody wanted to be in that pile because it meant you were expected to die. People went to that pile if we knew we could not save them.

This hierarchy of the injured may seem totally barbaric, but we were already in such a different mental zone at that time that we learned to make those tough calls. I never feared death myself, but it made me question many things that I had learned about God from the boys' home. I became convinced that there was no Heaven or Hell. I thought for sure that when we died, that was it. We just ceased to exist. Heaven began to feel like a nice fairytale we choose to delude ourselves with.

Despite the fact that we were overseas for seven months, the war itself only lasted about ten days. When we had secured the city and achieved victory, the Iraqis quickly signed a ceasefire agreement, but we learned how ruthless they were. As we went through the city destroying all of their old Russian military tanks and weaponry, we saw that the Iraqis had marked most of them with crescent moons to make us think they were medical vehicles. Some of them were booby-trapped to explode. When we would look in other vehicles to see if there were any injured people, we would find burned-up carcasses left inside.

Our final station was on the outskirts of Kuwait City. I badly wanted to go inside the city after the ceasefire to see what it looked like, but only our Special Forces and senior officers were allowed in to clean out any lingering insurgents. The night they liberated the city, we could hear music blaring from miles away. We were so jealous. After the ceasefire was signed, hundreds of thousands of Iraqis came to us wanting to become enemy prisoners of war rather than return home to Saddam's regime. We were overwhelmed by insurgents begging us to take them because they knew we would treat them better than their own countrymen would. It was crazy how ill-equipped and poorly taken care of they were. We eventually had to stop taking EPOWs because we did not have the resources to help everybody.

It was really sad that they were so terrified to return home after fighting for their country. At the same time, I couldn't wait to return home. I was so ready to get back home to my wife.

A few weeks after the war ended and we were debriefed, we flew home to California. Buses picked us up from the airport, and we were met with a ticker-tape parade that rivaled Times Square on New Year's Eve. People were lined up along the roads cheering for us, throwing confetti, and handing us pizza and ice-cold beers. It was awesome to see the support our country was showing our military, because the Vietnam veterans did not get such a generous homecoming. We still had several Marines who had served in Vietnam fighting in Desert Storm. My master sergeant was a Vietnam veteran, and he remembered people spitting on the soldiers as they returned home. I was glad he finally got the hero's welcome he deserved. Marines don't get to choose their battles. No one who serves in the military does. We took the oath to serve our country and protect our Constitution from all who threaten it—not just the "popular" enemies.

But coming home was a rough adjustment. I had seen things I couldn't unsee and, after seven months of constantly being on alert or attacked, garrison life was difficult to get used to again. A lot of guys struggled mentally after they came back. Any time a car back-fired or a jet flew overhead, we would hit the deck out of habit. It took a while to reassimilate.

Shortly afterward, my wife, Amy, got pregnant with our son, Jacob. We found out when we took a trip to Disneyland. That was a really freaky and cool time in our lives. Neither of us had ever planned on having a kid, but as soon as we found out she was pregnant, we were happy. It was a rough pregnancy because we were living in Twentynine Palms at the time, in the middle of the desert near Palm Springs. Jacob's was a pretty traumatic birth. I was in the room with Amy, and she started hemorrhaging. Jacob's face was turning blue as he emerged from the birth canal. The doctors were freaking out. I was freaking out. They kicked me out of the room as they rushed Amy into emergency surgery and Jacob off to NICU to try to get him breathing again. As I waited, praying, I was terrified they were both going to die. After what seemed like an eternity, the doctor came out and told me that both my wife and my newborn son were going to be fine. I was so relieved.

I loved being a dad to Jacob. He was so tiny and perfect. My Marine buddies were absolutely fascinated by him. It was surreal because we still often felt like kids ourselves, yet here I was with an actual kid. It took Amy some time to recover from the birth, so I would stay up with Jacob at night so she could sleep. I would fix myself a bowl of cereal and put on old kung fu movies while Jacob slept on my chest. It was just the most amazing time.

Years later, as my marriage started to get rocky, I wanted to be off playing Marine rather than taking care of my family. The Marines always came first in my life. Given my own upbringing, I had never valued family, so when my attempts to save my marriage failed, I had an affair. When Amy and I got divorced, she took Jacob. That killed me.

I know I did a disservice to my son in his formative years. I often wish I had been a better dad to him, like I'd been to my football players. I didn't begin to appreciate the importance of family until I married Denise after a second marriage failed. Despite the fact that I had been in love with her since I first laid eyes on her, it took a long time for the stars to align for us.

CHAPTER 8

LOVE AT FIRST SIGHT
... AGAIN

(With Denise Kennedy)

I couldn't share the sequence of crazy events in my relationship with Denise without including her, so we're going to tell this bit of our story together.

Denise: I'd like to start by going back to our first meeting. You told your side of that exchange, but you have to understand that I was a painfully shy child. Joe likes to make our first meeting sound like this big Hollywood romantic moment where time slowed down and all that—

Joe: Because it did!

Denise: I don't remember it that way. What I remember is that I was playing in the dirt, minding my own business, when all of a sudden, this strange boy with long curly hair was asking me to marry him. I was just thinking, *What?!* Then I started thinking, *Oh my word, he lives just down the road from me.* I was creeped out. I just wanted to run away. I was still at the age where boys were gross and probably had cooties.

Joe: I was only nine years old, too. I had always thought girls were cute, but this was the first time I had seen a girl and it left me speechless. I had no words. I was completely mesmerized. She was not at all amused.

Denise: No, I was not. Plus, he was a hoodlum. He was always in trouble. But eventually my stepsister, Corey, and I started hanging out with Joe and Ty.

Joe: We did everything together, and Ty and I were always competing to see who would win Denise's heart. We were both madly in love with her the entire time we were growing up. We would play in the woods, have ice fights, hang out at each other's houses, and watch *Creep Show*.

I'll never forget the first time I got to hold Denise's hand. We were fourteen and a bunch of us were watching *Creep Show* in Denise's bedroom. I remember Ty got mad and left because he saw I was holding her hand. I was on cloud nine. She was the popular yuppie girl, and she was so good, too. Meanwhile, Corey was more like me—always in trouble. Corey and I actually got along really well because of that.

When I was thirteen, I finally got Denise to go out with me. I think I asked her, "Hey, would you be my girl?" or something like that. I didn't know what I was doing, but she wrote me a note back that said "Yes, I'll be your girlfriend." We went on one date. Her mom made spaghetti, and that was the first time I ever kissed her. We were holding hands walking down the side of the driveway. My hands were clammy and sweaty. I'm sure it was gross. I stopped, and I was like, *I'm just gonna do it*. I didn't want to ask her first or give her any chance to shoot me down, so I just kissed her. She thinks I'm exaggerating when I say I saw fireworks going off in my head, but I started seeing all these bright dots flashing in my brain because I was kissing the girl I had adored since I was nine. It was one of those really long, awkward kisses, but it blew my mind.

Then she turned and ran up the driveway. I had to sit down for a minute because my brain was just fried. I was dizzy. (Even today when I kiss Denise, it still makes me dizzy.) I remember looking up after our first kiss and seeing her run away. I started panicking. *Oh no? Was it bad? Did I just mess everything up?* I had no idea what went wrong.

Denise: Remember, I was this "good girl." I was not nearly as experienced as he was at the whole dating and kissing thing. I didn't know what to do.

Joe: I thought I had just ruined things with Denise. I think she ended up writing me a letter a few days later apologizing for running off.

Denise: Yeah, because that was how we communicated. We wrote letters to each other all the time. That's how I really got to know Joe, because he was in and out of foster homes and then at the boys' home. And even when he was in the Marines, we would still write to each other.

Joe: She would write me these letters that were four and five pages long, and I would save them until I could read them alone at night after curfew.

Denise: I think we saved most of those letters. Didn't you just find one the other day?

Joe: Yeah, it had one of those Now and Later candies in it and it said, "I want to kiss you Now and Later." It was so sweet.

Denise: So cheesy!

Joe: The second time that Denise and I briefly dated as teenagers, I remember I was holding her hand, and I think I even knelt down like it was this big proposal. She was standing above me like she was on this pedestal—as she had always been in my mind—and I asked her to be my girl. She actually looked me in the eyes and said, "Yeah."

I pulled her towards me, and we kissed right there on the steps. Those were the only two times we kissed growing up.

That didn't last long, though, because her stupid girlfriends messed it up. I hated those girls. They were so mean. Denise had invited me to this Catholic Youth thing she went to on Wednesday nights. I went, and as soon as I entered the building, these three girls came and blocked my path. They had their hands on their hips, and they were just staring daggers at me. They said, real snooty-like, "Denise doesn't want to talk to you. She's too good for you, and she doesn't want to be your girlfriend anymore." They said it *so* loud that the entire room went quiet. Imagine a couple hundred teens and all the commotion that entails, and it all went silent as the grave. Everyone was staring at me. You could hear a pin drop. I was mortified. I looked over at Denise, and she wouldn't even make eye contact. I was so mad and embarrassed that I turned and left.

Denise: It was horrible. I was sitting at the opposite end of the room on one of the couches they had set up for us, and—oh, I just felt so bad for the longest time. I had *never* told them to go and do that, but I was way too insecure to make a scene and try to fix it. I think I wrote him that night to apologize, but pretty soon after that, he went to the boys' home.

Looking back on all of that now, it's crazy because I think I knew at some point when we were growing up that Joe was the one. Even though we only dated those two brief times, there was always this connection between us. I didn't know how to deal with that back then because he was always in trouble. But then he would show so much intuition and wisdom in spite of his rebellion. It was confusing!

Joe: You think I was wise back then?

Denise: In some ways! But I was scared. I was in no position to be vulnerable with Joe even if I did feel this genuine, deep love. The thought of loving Joe terrified me. He was so different from me, that

I was always thinking, *How would this ever work?* It was like we were from opposite sides of the railroad tracks, but there always was this deep, undeniable connection. Nobody else ever understood me or saw me as my true self other than Joe. And he still liked me. I didn't have to explain myself or try to change myself. It was such a remarkable feeling. That's why, after my girlfriends broke up with him for me at the youth event, I felt such an intense sadness and loss. It broke my heart, but I was too insecure to go against the popular girls that I was friends with.

Joe: And then you started dating that gay guy.

Denise: I didn't know he was gay at the time.

Joe: I instantly knew he was gay. He went to the same church, and we all went in the same group to school dances together. But this was the 1980s when being gay was *not* cool. Things were totally different.

Denise: Yeah, it was very much still taboo. I just remember he was a really good friend, and he made me feel safe.

Joe: Me, too. When I was in the Marines and found out from your cousin that you were living with a guy, I was jealous until she told me you were living with *that* guy. I knew nothing would ever happen between you two, so if you had to live with a guy, I was thrilled it was him.

Denise: When I first started dating him, we just clicked. I didn't realize why at first, but there was an intimacy between us that wasn't about the physical. We could talk about anything and everything. I didn't have to worry about intimate expectations with him. We just hit it off. When I graduated, he was living out of town, and he asked me to move with him. I didn't have a job or anything, but I so badly wanted to get out of Bremerton that I said yes. It was totally on a whim.

Joe: We were still writing letters to each other even when I shipped off to Japan. I bought Denise this really cool leather jacket while I was over there, and she sent me pictures of her wearing it. The summer that I came home for leave, I had bought a ring and was going to propose to Denise. Her aunt picked me up at the ferry, and I showed her the ring I had picked out. Then she told me that Denise had moved away with that guy. I was heartbroken. I threw the ring off the side of the ferry into the Puget Sound, and I ended up hooking up with her cousin, Amy, that summer.

Amy had hung around with all of us while we were growing up, so we had always been good friends. She was cute and funny, and we spent that whole summer together. I thought we were just having a good time, but when she brought me back to the airport to fly back to Japan, she proposed to me. We were saying goodbye, and she asked, "Should we get married?" I looked at her like, "Do you want to get married?" She said she did, so we were kind of engaged from that point.

When I was back in Okinawa, Amy was busy planning our future together. Meanwhile, I was freaking out going, *Holy crap, what did I just do?* It's not that I didn't want to marry her—just that the whole idea of marriage freaked me out. I was still so immature. I didn't know if I was ready to be a husband. It was half-exciting, half-terrifying. It must have been obvious that I didn't want to get married because, even at the courthouse, one of our friends who we asked to be a witness threatened to tackle me if I tried to leave without marrying her. Even though I didn't want to get married, I really did love Amy and was too nice of a guy to not go through with it.

At first, marriage was great. We had a kid. We loved each other. It was fun being newlyweds, and we had eleven wonderfully happy years together. But then I started getting deployed more, and I went overseas to fight in Kuwait. I was always putting my job ahead of family. Shortly after Jacob was born, I got orders to go to Japan. I fully expected Amy and Jacob to come with me, but all of Amy's family was in Washington. I could either go for three years with them or a year without them. Amy didn't want to move, so I spent a year in Japan away from them.

While I was away, she started seeing another guy. She told me over the phone that she wanted a break. I was so upset that I asked for emergency leave. I flew home, desperate to fix things with her. We went to counseling, and things got better for a while. We moved to Boise when I was stationed there, and for four years, things were really good again. We bought our first house; Jacob was in school. Then I got orders to move to Lewiston. Amy didn't want to move. She had a good job in Boise and we had a cool life there—but when you're in the military, moving comes with the territory. I wasn't about to retire, so we made the decision to live separate lives. I would move to Lewiston and come back to Boise on weekends. That was the beginning of the end of us.

I ended up cheating on her. I had been seeing this other woman for six months. It was eating me up, the fact that we were living separate lives and I was being unfaithful. I finally came clean to Amy. I'll never forget her reaction. She said, "Oh, thank goodness." That was not at all the reaction I was expecting. "I thought you were going to ask me for a divorce," she explained. I thought maybe she hadn't heard me correctly.

"For Pete's sake, I'm living with another woman!"

She said, "Yeah, okay."

Okay? That's when I knew I had to get a divorce. I realized that she didn't love me as much as she loved the idea of being married. So we got a divorce, and I got remarried to the other woman.

Denise: Meanwhile, I had no idea that he ever intended to propose on that trip. I was still in my relationship when Amy called me to tell me she was getting married. I was like, "Oh, that's great. To whom?" She told me, "Joey Kennedy."

I obviously couldn't say how I really felt—I probably didn't know what I really felt at that time—so I did my best to put on a good face and be happy for them. But family gatherings were kind of weird after that because I had to see them all the time.

Joe: One of the worst, most awkward moments in my marriage to Amy was when Denise started having problems with her boyfriend. Amy was trying to give her advice on how to be sexier for him, and every fiber of my being was just screaming inside. It was like when a cat bristles up and all its hair stands up everywhere. I was thinking, *You are NOT telling Denise that she needs to be sexier for this guy! ARE YOU FREAKING KIDDING ME!* Denise was the most beautiful woman in the world. There was nothing wrong with her. It was simply never going to happen between the two of them.

Denise: Again, I didn't know he was gay at the time. I just knew things were getting really weird between us. We had been living together for a while, and even though there was no real physical attraction initially—and I had been okay with that—I was beginning to wonder if something was wrong with me. I felt even more insecure in myself and in my body because I couldn't understand why he found me so undesirable. Eventually, he told me that he was gay, and I was so relieved. It finally explained everything. After he came out, we finally broke up, and shortly thereafter, I married my first husband.

Joe: Denise was pregnant with her first child, Emily, around the same time that Amy and I had our son, Jacob.

Denise: We had three children together. Emily, Zach, and my youngest son, Ethan. It was not a healthy marriage. I tried to leave two times before I was finally successful.

Joe: I thought they were happily married. Because I had never stopped loving Denise, it drove me nuts when I would see her with her husband. At one family gathering when I was still married to Amy, her husband came up to me and point-blank asked, "Are you in love with my wife?" Before I could even stop myself, I just said: "Yes. I always have been." It just flew out of my mouth. His face turned dark and he said, "I'm not cool with that." I told him, "I don't care if you're cool with it or not. You're married to her. I'm married to Amy. So that's where we're at." I mean, I wasn't going to do anything. I knew I wasn't a great husband or father, but I still respected the institution of marriage at that point.

When I divorced Amy, it killed me that she got custody of Jacob. I only got to see him on certain holidays, so when I did get time with him, I tried to make sure we did the most fun things. My second wife, Elaine, wanted to have kids, but after losing Jacob in my divorce, I was not about to bring any more children into my messed-up life. That marriage only lasted about five years before I did the less-than-honorable thing and left.

Denise: After I decided to leave my ex-husband, I continued to work at Mervyn's, a department store where I'd worked for over a decade. My ex-husband and I still hadn't officially divorced yet, but we were living completely separate lives. I was working twelve-hour days at the store to support my three kids, and I finally came to the conclusion that I was okay with dying an old maid. I mean, I was in my late thirties, had three kids and a mountain of debt, I was working all the time and never home, and I had really low self-esteem. I thought, *Who in their right mind would want me?* I went out with some coworkers one night, and I was telling them all of this when I got a call from Joe.

Joe: Coincidence? Meanwhile, I was home on leave visiting Jacob. I was asking him what he had been doing, and he told me that he and Amy had just gone to Denise's birthday party. That caught my attention. "You still talk to Denise?" I asked. Denise was his second cousin, so of course he talked to her. He told me she was no longer with her husband, and in the meantime, my second marriage was falling apart, so I asked him, "Do you have her number?"

I had no idea what was going on with Denise or that she had just told her friends that she would be happy to die an old maid. I just called her up out of the blue to catch up, but when she answered, all those old feelings kept flooding back. We talked for three hours that night about everything and nothing. Before we hung up, I asked if I could see her. She told me that she was working late, but if I wanted to have dinner with her and her kids, I could come by after she got home.

Denise: Meanwhile, I'm thinking we're just gonna be two old friends catching up. I had zero interest in dating again.

Joe: I drove over to her house the next night, and Emily answered the door. Denise was in sweats and a hoodie, her hair was down, she had no makeup on. She looked like she was ready to go to bed, but I kid you not, when she looked up at me with those big, beautiful brown eyes, I flashed back to the first time I saw her at nine years old. It was like time slowed down again, and I was once again looking at the woman I'd loved my entire life.

She looked so beautiful to me as she got up out of her La-Z-Boy recliner to give me a hug. She looked so exhausted that I asked her if she wanted to call it off and just take a rain check so she could go get some sleep, but she went, "No, no. Stay. It's just been a really long day."

I offered to cook spaghetti because it was one of the only things I knew how to cook. Also because it was what her mom had cooked for us on our first date when we were thirteen. I was excited just to be having dinner with Denise, but the whole time I was cooking, I kept randomly wondering, *What would happen if I kissed her neck?* Her hair was pulled up in a messy bun with wispy hairs falling down her long neck. I wanted to kiss her so bad, but I thought *That would probably be weird. No, don't blow it, Joe. Just be cool.* I'm having this long argument with myself over what to do, because I just wanted to kiss her so bad. The whole night I was thinking of romance—

Denise: And I was so *not*. I mean, yeah, there was some lingering chemistry between us, but I didn't know if it was just wishful thinking.

Joe: We ate dinner together and, as she walked me out to my truck afterward, I thought, *I'm probably never going to get this chance again.* I mean, what was I really going to lose? So I leaned in and kissed her. When she pulled away, she kind of looked at me and cocked her head a bit to the side. It was adorable. Her eyebrows were raised up really high, and she was blushing. She asked, "Can I call you later?" From that point on, we talked every night for hours. I would drive three hours both ways from where I was stationed in Oregon to come visit her on weekends.

Denise: The whole thing kind of surprised me at first, but the more I thought about it, the more I thought, *This could work.* And the more we talked, the more it was like nothing had changed between us. But he was still married to Elaine. They hadn't finalized their divorce yet, and I was still technically married to my husband. Even though I had left, I had no money to get a divorce. It took us a little time to work everything out.

Joe: I was in such a hurry to get married. I didn't want Denise to change her mind. I had been wanting this since I was nine! For the first time, we were both in a position where we could do this. I think I proposed to her pretty quickly after we started dating.

Denise: I got the paperwork, and two weeks later we got married on May 20, 2005.

Joe: I was still in the Marines. We were now in two wars post–9/11 with Afghanistan and Iraq, and I so badly wanted to deploy overseas.

Denise: Yeah, I was not thrilled about that, but it was what he had trained for and what he loved, so I was not going to stand in his way. I told him that he needed to do what he thought he needed to do.

Joe: I had put my papers in to go to Afghanistan or Iraq, and I was told that my company wouldn't get deployed because I was the only guy who had been in combat and could teach it. They needed me stateside. I was acting first sergeant, so unless my sergeant major retired or was killed in Afghanistan, there was no place for me to go over there.

After several months, I got called in and told that the commanding officer, sergeant major, and first sergeant had all gone out looking for action in Kabul. You *never* put all your commanding guys in one vehicle. *Never.* There should always be a designated survivor. But they were all out there riding around in one of the armored Humvees, and the first sergeant decided to pull the blast window down so he could take a better picture of an improvised explosive device on the ground. Again, absolute stupidity. While he had the window down, the bomb detonated, killing him. That's when they told me I was being called up. I was so excited. I called Denise to tell her, and she seemed weirdly out of it. I figured she was tired or upset that I was going to be gone because she kept trying to hurry me off the phone.

Denise: I was actually in the hospital when he called. I had been feeling really weird the night before when I was closing up the store. I felt like the side of my face was all droopy, and I was having trouble articulating words. One of the assistants who was closing up with me noticed that my whole left side was just hanging, and he told me, "Denise, I think you need to go to the hospital." My head was really hurting. I'd always suffered with migraines, so I just wrote it off to that, but he kept telling me that my face was droopy. One of my other coworkers saw me and told me to go to the hospital right then and there. As I drove to the hospital, I noticed I could not move my left arm. I walked into the emergency room, and they immediately rushed me back. I was still being observed and having tests run when Joe called me, so I told him to call me later.

Joe: When she finally told me that she was in the hospital. I was shocked. She told me that the doctors said she had a transient ischemic attack (a TIA or mini-stroke), but that I should go ahead and do what I thought was best regarding my deployment. The next day, I marched straight into my commanding officer's office and handed in my retirement notice. I didn't even give it a second thought. I was so worried about Denise. Nothing else mattered. I hurried home as soon as I got permission to leave the base.

Denise: I had to go see all these specialists after I was released from the hospital. I went to see a neurologist, and he told me that my blood vessels were so restricted that I wasn't getting proper blood flow. I would either have to have tubes put into the blood vessels to open them up, or they could put me on anti-seizure meds. I chose the latter and was on the anti-seizure meds for several years. At the time, I was also trying to finish my associate's degree at the local community college, and I remember being frustrated that I couldn't function as well as I had before the stroke. The left side of my body was weaker for a while, and it seemed like my emotions were all over the place.

Joe: From my perspective, it seemed like she had abandoned all rational thought. She quit her job at Mervyn's on a whim. She had been working there for twenty years and was a store manager making big bucks, plus yearly bonuses. She didn't consult with me or even mention that she had been considering it. She just came home from work and told me that she'd quit her job. She didn't even negotiate a severance package. It was as if the logical side of her brain had shut down and she was unable to process anything deeper than these whims and emotional roller coasters.

Denise: I couldn't figure out what the heck was wrong with me. I know I was acting like a complete mental case, but I couldn't control it. I felt like I was trying to communicate, but it was so frustrating that I would just start crying.

Joe: I do not do well with tears. We went from being totally happy to her crying all the time and trying to sabotage our marriage.

Denise: I can't even explain why, but I wanted to destroy our marriage. It was terrible. It wasn't even conscious. I felt so unworthy of someone caring for me and doting on me as much as Joe was. I felt out of control of my own mind.

Joe: She was going to church at the time. I still was going through my relatively agnostic phase, but after months of this, I was desperate to try anything to save our marriage. I started going to church with her, but I didn't really want to be there. I didn't really agree with the pastor or like the sermons. However, as things got worse between me and Denise, I began sitting in church thinking *What the heck are we gonna do?*

We had just had the first really big fight of our marriage one morning before church, and I was terrified I was going to lose Denise. They always had altar calls at the church, and Denise would squeeze my elbow each time they had one and ask if I wanted to go down. I never did, but this day, I was at the end of myself. Things had gotten so bad between us that I didn't know what else to do. All of a sudden, I felt this unmistakable force drawing me to the altar. I felt God pulling me out of my seat and down the center aisle. I didn't have control of my body as I went down to the altar, sobbing and praying, *God, if You give Denise back to me and help everything work out, I will give You the rest of my life.* It was like an out-of-body experience. In that moment, I completely surrendered my entire everything to God.

Not even joking, *that day* everything changed between us.

Denise: It gave me so much security to see Joe finally go down to the altar and surrender to God. I felt like I had been the spiritual leader of our family up until then, which was out of order biblically. When Joe went down to the altar, he became the spiritual leader of the family. He had never surrendered to anything before. Because he was a tough Marine, he saw any kind of surrender as weakness. To see him surrender wholeheartedly to God was a huge thing for me in our marriage. I could trust him in a way that I had never been able to before because I knew he was going to put God first. When he came back from that altar call, he even looked different. He held himself differently.

Joe: We went from hardly communicating to both of our defenses completely dropping—all her past baggage, all my crap—everything just went away, and we were able to connect like we had never connected before. God had stripped away all of the bull until there was just the real, vulnerable me standing there, and Denise was suddenly like the old Denise. She was rational and deep-thinking again. As soon as I surrendered to God, He miraculously fixed everything between us. Again, I'm sure it was all coincidence, right?

CHAPTER 9

A Father to the Fatherless

Before all the lawsuit stuff happened, I loved coaching. Even with the lawsuit, I still loved coaching—it just got a lot more challenging after the school district started telling me what I could and couldn't do. Those first seven seasons, however, were a blast. I got to coach some of the finest young men, many of whom I've stayed friends with. We had some of the craziest times and a lot of real, hard life lessons.

The first season I coached, there was a kid named Shawn. He was maybe 145 pounds soaking wet—a totally unassuming kid, but I could tell he was really smart. There was just something about him. During training camp, I told him, "You're gonna be the team captain." He said, "Me? I'm not popular. I'm not even that great an athlete." To this day, I still can't name exactly what it was about him. It was almost like God smacked me upside the head like Reverend Shoals used to do with his giant ring and said, "Shawn's the one." I started pouring into him and building the team around him. I saw great leadership potential in him, and he exceeded my expectations as our team captain.

Early on that first season when I was coaching Shawn, he approached me after a game, and said, "Hey, Coach, the team is really tired and really beat up. I think we need to take Saturday off."

"What, the whole team?" I asked. That was a highly unusual ask.

"Yeah," he said. "I'm not going to be there. My grandparents are coming into town, and there's just a lot going on with myself and the team. You know me, I want to be a team leader, but if I can't be here, I think we should have a break."

As my team captain, I was trusting he knew what's best for the team, so I said, "Alright, good enough."

I had gotten a one-game suspension for yelling at the referees the previous game, so I was sitting with Denise in the stands. A woman in front of us was screaming *so loudly* during the game that I tapped her on the shoulder and asked, "Which kid is yours?"

She pointed at Shawn.

"I love that kid," I told her.

She looked at me funny. "You know Shawn?"

"Well, yeah, I'm Coach Kennedy."

"*You're* Coach Kennedy?" she asked, surprised to see me in the stands instead of on the field. I told her I was the coach who had thrown a tantrum after a bad call the last game.

"Oh, that was *you*?" she asked.

"Yes ma'am," I admitted. "Not my proudest moment."

We started talking, and I told her, "I hope Shawn had a good weekend with your parents."

She looked at me funny a second time. "What?"

"Yeah," I said, "Shawn told me your parents were in town."

"Coach, my parents are dead," she answered.

God's got a funny sense of humor. Had I not been suspended, I never would have sat next to Shawn's mother at that game and caught him in a bald-faced lie. Shawn had looked me in the face and told me a straight-up fib so the whole team could goof off. Coincidence, right? Oh, was he going to pay. You don't lie to Coach.

I decided to get creative.

The Bremerton football field is shaped like a sunken bowl. On one side are the visitors' bleachers, with an open field behind them at the top. On the other side are the home team bleachers with the words BREMERTON KNIGHTS spelled out at the top in letters so big you could easily see them from the upper field across the stadium.

One practice, I was standing in the upper field and called for Shawn to come over to me. He ran up the side of the hill. "Yes, Coach?"

"Run down to the bleachers and tell me what that first letter is up there."

"It's a B, Coach," he answered without thinking about it.

"Are you sure about that?" I asked. "I think you need to go check and make sure."

I made him run down the hill, past the visitors' bleachers, across the football field, and all the way up the home bleachers to the very top row to check the letter. After he checked it, he had to run all the way back to me.

"It's definitely a B, Coach," he informed me.

"Okay. How about the next letter?" I asked. "Go back there and tell me what the second letter is."

Shawn ran back down the hill, across the field, up the bleachers, checked the letter, down the bleachers, across the field, and then back up the hill to me.

"It's an R, Coach."

I made him run and tell me every letter spelling out "Bremerton Knights," one by one. I ran him ragged. It seemed to last forever, but he knew exactly what he was paying for. I never caught another player telling me a bald-faced lie again.

Aside from that one shenanigan, Shawn was the greatest kid. He became known as "Mr. Football." He was everything we wanted in a team captain. To this day, the coaches will still say, "Man, I wish we had another Shawn." I went to his high school graduation, his college graduation, and even his wedding. He was the first kid that I really was able to mentor.

But there were great stories and many great kids every year. Another of my standout guys was a kid called Mahoney. He was a lot like Shawn. He went from 5'8" to 6'3" really quickly. It took him some time to grow into himself. He would trip over his feet like an awkward deer learning to run, but he had a great arm and a lot of really good common sense when it came to playing football. We picked him to be our quarterback. He could handle himself in the pocket with grace far beyond his years, but he was always really hard on himself. If he threw an interception, he would beat himself up about it.

At the time, Mahoney was dating a girl who ended things with him right on the field, in front of all his teammates. It broke his heart. The other guys were all laughing at him. Nobody was respecting Mahoney—but he was not only their quarterback, he was a team captain. They had to respect the captains because if they didn't, our team structure would crumble. I knew I had to do something quick to help Mahoney earn back the respect of his teammates.

After mulling it over for a few minutes, I remembered something from my days in bootcamp that seemed applicable: My drill instructor, Salazar, caught us whining and complaining one day. We had a unit flag and, wherever we went, one of the guys would wave it proudly to show we were coming. When Salazar heard us whining and complaining, he got mad, threw our flag on the ground, and started telling us to stomp on it.

"Go ahead, stomp on it!" he yelled. "You obviously don't care about your platoon. Go ahead. You have my blessing. Stomp on your unit flag."

A bunch of the guys started yelling, "F this!" and began to stomp and spit on it.

"Screw this platoon!" one yelled.

As I watched, I started to get mad. I was thinking, *What are you guys doing? That's OUR platoon!* I felt pride in our platoon. It was who we were!

Salazar saw me standing back as the guys were stomping on the flag. He blew the whistle and said, "Kennedy, why aren't you stomping on the flag? I *order* you to go stomp on the flag!"

"No sir!" I announced. "This private will not disgrace his platoon by stepping on its flag."

Salazar marched over to me with his wide-brimmed hat, the brim hitting me in the nose.

"You think you're better than everyone else?" he taunted. "I gave you a direct order. Go stomp on the flag, Kennedy!"

"Sir, no sir!" I stood firm. "This private will not disgrace his platoon by stepping on its flag."

"YOU DISOBEY AN ORDER, KENNEDY?" Salazar snarled and spat in my face.

"No disrespect, sir, but this private will not disgrace his platoon by stepping on its flag," I repeated.

Suddenly, I could see everyone else start going, "Yeah, I'm not gonna do that anymore."

They began, one by one, to back away from the flag and stand at attention beside me. As I watched them come join me, I saw

Salazar looking at me with a smirk that said, *Yeah, Kennedy. You passed that test.*

I figured I had to do something like that to get the football team back on Mahoney's side, so I took one of our practice sleds out of the shed and started making trips back and forth from our weight room, stacking the weights on it. I must have loaded close to a thousand pounds on that thing. After a few trips, the kids started to notice I was up to something. A few asked me what I was doing, but I ignored them. I just kept stacking the weights on the sled. Usually, I was always energetic and engaging with them, but this time I was dead silent.

It took me about an hour to stack all the weights up on that sled. I gave the whole team a water break and let them sit in the shade to cool down—everyone except Mahoney. By this time, nobody was talking, and everybody was watching me. After I had set it all up, I called Mahoney over.

"Yes, Coach?"

"You're a team captain, right?" I asked.

"Yes, Coach."

"How's your team responding to you?"

"What do you mean, Coach?"

"Do you think you have the respect of your team, Mahoney?"

"Uhhhhh . . . no, Coach."

"Since you're a team captain," I said in front of everyone, "you need to be able to lead the team, and I'm afraid you're just not cutting it. If you want to lead this team, you ought to be able to move the whole team in any one direction. I want you to grab that rope, and I want you to pull that sled ten yards, and we're gonna sit here and watch."

I knew there was no chance that Mahoney could get that sled to budge, but he ran over, picked up the rope, and started pulling on it.

It didn't move. He was struggling and struggling, and the team was watching, going, "What the heck?"

I turned to the team. "What do you think of Mahoney, guys? Look at him. He's pretty weak, right? What a wimp. Man, he sucks. YOU SUCK, MAHONEY! Isn't that right, guys?"

A couple of the guys started clowning on him, "Yeah!"

I kept on. "He's a joke, right? Let's all laugh at Mahoney. He can't even freaking do this by himself. What kind of team captain is that?"

More of the kids joined in on the bashing. They thought it was awesome to rib on the team captain. I egged it on. "Come on! Let's all laugh at Mahoney. Come on, everybody, laugh it up!"

Then the kids started getting uncomfortable. Meanwhile, Mahoney was struggling, throwing every ounce of his strength into trying to get that sled to move. It wasn't going anywhere.

Mahoney's face was bright red. He was embarrassed because he was right there and could hear everything. He looked like he wanted to die right on that spot. His feet were digging ruts into the field, trying to get that sled to budge. He was doing everything he could. I noticed a couple of the players starting to get restless like they wanted to get up and help, so I turned to them and said, "Nobody help him. If anybody gets up to help Mahoney, the whole team is going to pay. He's the team captain. *He's* supposed to lead this team."

By this point, Mahoney was crying. Tears were just streaming down his face. His hands were starting to blister and bleed from the rope burns. Finally, I looked over and asked, "Where are my other captains?"

We usually had three or four captains at one time, so they raised their hands. I said, "You guys are supposed to be backing him up. You're supposed to have his back at *all* times. Get out there and help. The rest of you, just sit here and watch."

The other captains got up and grabbed the rope with Mahoney. Even with the extra manpower, they could barely inch the sled forward. These were the biggest and strongest players on the team, and they were all struggling. It was hot, and they were dripping with sweat. The whole exercise was going on way too long, and the other coaches were starting to get concerned.

I turned back to the rest of the players. "This is your team," I said. "You've got one guy who can't do everything by himself. You've got all the team captains here, and they can't even do it. We're gonna sit right here and see how long it takes them to move this sled ten yards. That's all they've got to do. Just ten yards."

Finally, one of the kids stood up and shouted, "Eff this, Coach! You can kick my butt, but I'm gonna help them!"

He ran over to help. Then another kid got up, and another, and another. One by one, this huge wave of kids ran over to help pick up the rope. The sled took off like a bullet as it flew past the goal line, and they all landed in a heap. Mahoney and the other captains were exhausted and their hands were all torn up, but it was one of those defining moments. They had earned back the respect of the team, and the team had rallied behind their captains.

I looked at them all and said, "*That's* what it's like to be a team."

Every year there would be at least one defining moment like that, but aside from that, we had an awful lot of fun too.

One year, there was a kid named Price. I recruited him from the marching band. He had never played football before, but he was a pretty good-sized kid. I would see him on the field practicing with the band, and one day I asked him if he ever thought about playing football. He tried out for the team and ended up becoming another one of our captains.

During one game, I noticed that something seemed out of place. I looked over and saw Price stuffing something into his waistband. I didn't know what he was hiding as the guys were lining up, ready for the snap. The other team was filled with giant dudes. They were ready to beat the crap out of us, when Price reached into his pants, pulled out a burrito, slowly took a giant bite, and then passed it across the line of scrimmage to the player facing off against him. The other guy stared at it for a moment, totally confused, but then reached out, grabbed the burrito, and took a bite. They went back and forth several times. None of the other coaches had any idea what was going on. Price had totally thrown the defense off their game with the burrito. It was just such a weird, awesome moment.

Another time, we had a kid we called Germany because he was an exchange student from Germany. He was fascinated by American football, and he wanted to try out for the team. I'd tell him, "Germany, go run ten."

He would look at me and say, "Ten what?"

"Ten yards."

"What's a yard?"

"Oh . . . it's like ten meters," I explained, forgetting Europeans used the metric system.

Germany loved the game of football. He absolutely loved the idea of whacking people, and I really wanted to get him to score a touchdown while he was with us. We must have tried six times one game to get him to score a touchdown. The whole team wanted it so badly for him that it became a free for all. He never did score one, but we made up for it in other ways.

During one game, I pulled him aside and said, "Hey, Germany, you're gonna be team captain today."

"Okay, Coach!"

"Here's the catch," I explained, "You can only speak German. You speak no English, got it?"

"But I do speak English, Coach," he argued.

"Not today. Today you only speak German. Understand?"

"Yes, Coach."

I turned to one of my other players, a kid called Dillon, and I told him, "Dillon, you're the translator. Germany's going to call out all the plays in German, and you're going to translate, okay?"

The kids were pumped about that prank. They went out onto the field, the referee did the introduction, and Germany started chattering away in German. Dillon was translating the calling of the coin toss. It was complete and utter nonsense. Meanwhile, the ref looked so confused. He turned to me and mouthed, "What the heck? He doesn't speak English!"

I shrugged at him like, "Nope."

We kept that going the entire game. Afterward, we told the ref, "Oh yeah, you know that German kid? He speaks perfect English."

It was hilarious because it intimidated the crap out of the other team to hear a kid yelling in German. He took it so seriously the entire game.

Perhaps the funniest story from my eight seasons of coaching involved a shopping cart. I would always run with my team. We had a five-mile course that I had mapped out that went around downtown Bremerton. On the way, we would run past a Safeway grocery store.

Once, we noticed two shopping carts sitting in the parking lot a long distance from the Safeway. Being good, upstanding citizens, we decided to divide the team in two and have a race to return the shopping carts. I put one of my biggest linemen in my cart, and the other team put someone in their cart, and the race was on.

We were pushing the shopping carts across gravel, which was ridiculous to begin with. It was a bumpy ride for our passengers. Between the gravel field and the Safeway parking lot was a big drainage ditch. We were running full-out as we approached it. I was thinking, *We can make this*. So I pushed with everything I had as we went down into the ditch—but I failed to take into account the lip on the other side. The cart's front wheels hit the embankment and catapulted me into the air. I hung onto the shopping cart for dear life, just like I had with the camel in Kuwait, as I flew like a trapeze artist end over end, still holding onto the shopping cart, before landing flat on my back. The lineman was ejected mid-air, like a sack of potatoes. I landed eight to ten feet from the launch point, right in the middle of the road. The wheel of the shopping cart hit me right in the groin as it landed on top of me.

Now, I have been beaten within an inch of my life, hit by a car, almost blown up in the Middle East, fought professionally (and unprofessionally) most of my life, and played Marine Corps football like I had a death wish—so when I tell you I had never been hit that hard in my life, I'm not kidding.

The other assistant coach, Brandon Nall, who enjoyed these shenanigans like I did, ran over to ask if I was okay. I was so out of it, I sat up and said, "What just happened?"

The other players were laughing and shouting, "Whoa, that was so cool!"

I asked Brandon to help me up. As he pulled me to my feet, someone went, "Coach, you're bleeding!"

I looked down and saw blood stains all around my groin. I started feeling around to make sure I still had all my equipment. I put my hand down my shorts, and it came away slicked in blood.

One of my players thought he would be a smart aleck and tell me, "Hey, Coach! Just rub some dirt on it"—something I had learned in the Marines and always told my players when they complained about minor injuries.

We were about a mile away from the school. Common sense was telling me to call an ambulance and go to the hospital, but there is a line between brave and stupid, and I still had no idea where it was. I wasn't about to wimp out in front of my team. I told Brandon to just give me a second, and I would walk the rest of the way with them.

As I tried to walk, my leg kept going out from under me. I had to drag it back the whole mile and a half back to the school like dead weight. We finally made it back, and I waited to make sure all the kids got cleaned up and went home. After everyone left, Brandon asked me if I was alright. I told him, "Man, just help me get to my truck, okay?"

I drove home, but when I pulled into my driveway, I could not physically get myself out of the truck. I was in so much pain, I called Denise to see if she was home. Thankfully she was.

"Hey, can you come help me out of the truck?" I asked.

"What did you do *now*?"

"Just, please come help me," I pleaded.

"Where are you?"

"In the driveway."

She came out and helped me out of the truck. I was in sorry shape as I limped up the stairs, having to put most of my weight on her.

"Honey, you've got to tell me straight-up, how bad is it?" she asked.

I dropped my blood-soaked drawers, and she exclaimed, "Oh my God! You ripped your sack! There's a big tear in it!"

She paused for a minute to take a closer look, and then asked, "Why is there dirt—Joe, TELL ME YOU DID *NOT* RUB DIRT IN IT!"

"Well—"

"I don't even know what to do with you," she said, exasperated. I refused to go to the hospital. I cleaned myself up as best I could. I had a blood blister the size of my forearm that ran all the way from my groin down to my knee. It was so big I could run my hand along it and see the blood pool in one direction and then the other.

That story is still legend at Bremerton High School. Every year it would get even crazier the more it got passed around.

There were a lot of crazy stories—but there were also a lot of real-life coaching moments with my players. Many of the kids had really difficult home lives—single parents, incarcerated parents, or no parents, couch-surfing or homeless, no money for food or football gear, a lot of false pregnancies and a few real ones. A lot of them thought about joining the military after graduation and would come to me for advice. We would have a lot of serious conversations about life. Never once did I bring up God. I'm not that guy who feels the need to preach to everybody. Most of what I said and did was consistent with what the Bible teaches. I didn't need to use words; I just *did* it.

Bremerton has the highest poverty level in Kitsap County. There are ten other school districts in the county, but Bremerton is the most impoverished. A lot of kids were on the free or reduced lunch program. It was the school where all the bad kids went, which is how I ended up there my senior year. I had gotten kicked out of all the other decent schools, including private Catholic ones. I knew what the Bremerton kids were facing because I had been one of them. I knew how to relate to them and how to get through to them.

One of my players had to work full-time, go to school full-time, play football, and support his family. That is a lot of real-life responsibility for a sixteen-year-old. I had another kid I would drive to the women's shelter after practice because his mom was staying there and they didn't have a car. One day, I caught a kid doing his laundry in the locker room because his family didn't have a washing machine and couldn't afford to go to the laundromat. Even though it was technically against the rules, I would leave boxes of detergent and fabric softener on top of the machines and pretend to look the other way so as not to embarrass him in front of the other guys or draw attention to his situation.

I had players stay at our house when their moms were strung out on drugs or their dads were on an abusive tear. Some of them didn't have money for food and would get their only meal at the school cafeteria, so I would take them out for pizza after the game because anyone with teenage boys knows they are always hungry. When a kid needed clothes, I would take him shopping and let him pick out what he needed. Thankfully, I was in a good place working at the shipyard and had a little discretionary income at the time to help out when I could.

A lot of these kids were trying to make something of themselves to better their lives. Having grown up in a similar situation, I knew what that was like. I wanted to help equip them, not just with the leadership tools and discipline they'd need after they graduated, but to help meet their most basic needs while I could.

That's why, when the prayer thing blew up, I didn't understand why everything else I had done for the team was being erased by a thirty-second knee at the fifty-yard line. I didn't beat the kids over the heads with a Bible or shove Jesus down their throats. I just tried to love on them through my actions and by being a steady presence in their lives.

On Senior Night—when graduating seniors honored the most influential person in their life by asking them to walk across the fifty-yard line with them—most students would choose their mom or grandma. However, it never failed that at least two or three students would choose me for that honor each year. I had a hard time with that. I've never been good at accepting praise, and that was so personal. The parents had raised the kids; I'd just come along to coach them in football. I never knew what to say when kids chose me over their own parents. It was cool to know that I'd had some sort of impact in their lives, but it was always weird. I remember when my son graduated high school. I thought for sure he was going to pick Amy or his stepdad as the most influential person in his life for Senior Night; I was floored when he picked me.

The most powerful moment I ever shared with a player was with a kid whose dad had been arrested for having inappropriate photos of underage girls. It was all over the news in Bremerton. His mother divorced his father, but the kid lived with merciless bullying from his peers. He was having a really rough time and wanted to quit the football team. He told me he had even thought about killing himself. One day, I took him out to the old boys' home where I used to live. It still looked exactly the same. Some of the same guys even still worked there.

I took my player to the exact spot that Reverend Shoals had taken me when I was his age. I told him to look across the valley and tell me what he saw on that same mountain. I pointed out that ugly tree that was *still there* on the barren, rocky mountainside. I put my arm around him and told him exactly what Reverend Shoals had told me that day: that tree had survived blizzards, mudslides, earthquakes, droughts—everything life had thrown at it. It wasn't pretty, but it was tough. It was a survivor. I told him he was like that tree.

He was blown away. He broke down, and I hugged him as he sat there and cried. It was cool to be able to share that with one of my guys and see it resonate with him like it had with me. I could see a look of hope wash over his face. He stuck it out and graduated from Bremerton, stayed on the football team, got a good job, and now has a family of his own. We're still good friends to this day.

This was the reality of my coaching career. It was loving these young men and trying to prepare them for life as adults. It wasn't about winning or losing, it wasn't about football, it wasn't even about the prayer. It was about being a father to the fatherless.

I never got to tell those stories in court. I had to sit quietly and let a bunch of lawyers talk for me and about me. Yeah, I prayed on the field. When the players joined, I didn't stop them. But that was thirty seconds twice a week that erased my whole career—eight seasons of moments like the ones I've just shared.

CHAPTER 10

CALLED TO FIGHT

After I got the first two directive letters from the Bremerton School District, one of my buddies called me out of the blue and told me I needed to get a lawyer. At that point, I still thought I could explain to the school district that this was all a big misunderstanding. I thought for sure if we could sit down face-to-face, we could work it all out.

But once the school district's attorneys got involved, Aaron, the superintendent, and I were no longer allowed to talk. That drove me nuts. We were friends. He was Denise's boss. We saw each other all the time, and now the school district's lawyers were telling him we couldn't have a simple conversation to clear up a matter that had been blown way out of proportion.

I had no interest in hiring lawyers, but my buddy, Coach Turso, kept telling me I needed to at least talk to his friend A. J. Ferate, a Bremerton alum. A. J. had seen a post Turso had put on Facebook about my situation and offered to talk to me. I had been getting calls from lawyers across the country wanting to represent me, but I wasn't taking any of them. But because of Turso's connection, I agreed to talk to A. J.

A. J. told me, "Coach, I hear you're in need of a bit of legal help. I just happened to be at a conference, and a group that specializes in religious liberty cases just did a presentation. I think these guys could really help you, and they're pro bono. Would you be interested in talking to them?"

I had to google what "pro bono" meant. I thought it had something to do with Sonny Bono.

A few days later I got a call from Hiram Sasser at First Liberty Institute in Plano, Texas.

"Is this Coach Joe Kennedy?" he asked.

"Yeah," I replied.

"Before we get started, I just have one question. Are you one of those religious nutjobs?"

I almost fell out of my chair laughing. I had expected any number of questions from an attorney, but not that one.

"No!" I stated. "I'm so far from it, it's not even funny."

"Good to know," he said, and the relief in his voice was palpable. "So, what's going on?"

I filled Hiram in on what had happened up to that point. He stopped me every so often to ask questions.

"So, you're telling me that you never asked these kids to pray with you?" he asked.

"No, sir."

"Never? Not even thinking you were being kind and extending an invitation?"

"No, sir." I repeated. "I didn't stop them if they wanted to join in, but I never wanted them to join me out there."

"You never made it seem like they wouldn't get to play if they didn't join you? Or that they might get preferential treatment if they did?"

I was an assistant coach. I wasn't the head coach or even defensive or offensive coach. I had absolutely *no* say in who played or didn't. The whole idea of the "pray to play" narrative that developed over the course of the case was laughable.

"No, man. It wasn't like that at all. It's a free country. They can do what they please, and I told them that from day one."

"Interesting," he said. "I think you have a case."

"Really?" I asked. Frankly, I was surprised. "So, what does that mean? What do we do?"

He explained my rights as an American, and he went into some long legal mumbo-jumbo about what the school's position was according to the courts and different precedents, etc. He told me he was going to send someone to meet with me and file a complaint with the Equal Employment Opportunity Commission.

We eventually filed the complaint, and the EEOC did an investigation, but we never wanted it to go to court. My attorney tried numerous times to meet with the superintendent to talk things out but couldn't even get the school district's lawyers to agree to meet with us about the *idea* of meeting with Aaron. It was frustrating. But after I got "Do Not Rehire" stamped on my annual review, we were left with no choice but to file the injunction against the Bremerton School District—a quicker process than a trial because the judge would issue a bench decision. No depositions would be taken, and no witnesses or jury would be called. Our only goal was to get me back on the field for my guys as quickly as possible.

I never asked for damages or back pay for the eight seasons of coaching that I would eventually miss. It was never about money—only the principle. The only thing I ever asked was to know if I was constitutionally allowed to pray on the football field. If the judge had said yes (or even no), I'd have complied. The law is the law, and I'm a law-abiding citizen. The problem was that nobody could give us a simple answer to what seemed like a straightforward question.

Going to court was an eye-opening experience. It's nothing like what you see on *Law & Order*. There's a whole lot of talking and very little justice. When we went to the district court in Seattle, my trial only lasted about an hour, but it seemed to go on for an eternity. I never got to speak on my own behalf. I watched helplessly as the district's lawyers spewed blatant lies about me, and my attorneys responded on my behalf. Many times, I wanted to jump up and scream, "That's crap!" and neck-punch somebody, but I couldn't. I had to sit there and behave when the Marine in me wanted to get up and fight! Thank God my local Seattle lawyer, Jeff Helsdon, was there to push my leg down so I couldn't jump up.

We asked the judge to grant a preliminary injunction so I could keep coaching until the trial was over, but the judge immediately denied that request. It killed me that I couldn't keep coaching. All I wanted was the opportunity to get back out on the field and have the freedom to take my thirty-second knee after the game. It didn't seem like a big ask.

The school district's lawyers later used a picture of me kneeling on the field, surrounded by a bunch of players, to try to prove their case against me. But what few people not directly involved with the trial seemed to notice is that those players weren't even my guys—they were all from Centralia, the team we were playing the night the photo was taken. When Bremerton's attorneys tried to use that photo against me as proof that I had coerced my players into praying, it was hilarious because none one of the players in that photo were even wearing our school's colors. (In fact, Centralia wasn't even in our district or league. It's on the other side of Washington, and Bremerton had played them in a nonconference game.) The reason is that none of my players could join me on the field that night because the Bremerton school district had just issued its first directives against me—so all of Centralia's players poured onto the field to pray with me instead. Nonetheless, the district used this picture in every single trial—and every time it came up, we pointed that out.

After the district court judge heard my case, he made an oral ruling from the bench, basically saying I had done nothing wrong. He even talked about how he prayed with his coaches when he played high school football and never thought anything of it. He talked about how prayer and football had been intertwined since the inception of the game, and how a football coach has more influence in a kid's life than any of the people sitting in the courtroom associated with the case that day. As I listened, I thought, *Holy crap, we might actually win.*

Boy, was I wrong. My jaw hit the floor when he concluded his soliloquy by saying that because of the current political climate, he couldn't grant my injunction. The *political* climate? Laws are laws. They are written down in black and white. Either what I did was against the law, or I was within my constitutional rights to pray. What did "the current political climate" have to do with anything?

That was his ruling from the bench. The judge never wrote anything down, so there was no official ruling—which is part of the reason the Supreme Court would eventually give us a second chance. He just denied the injunction with no explanation, so we appealed to the Ninth U.S. Circuit Court of Appeals. The complaint read:

> [Bremerton School District] publicly admitted that there is "no evidence" that students have ever been "coerced to pray with Coach Kennedy.". . . BSD further conceded that Coach Kennedy's religious expression is "fleeting"—lasting no more than thirty seconds—and that no student, parent, or member of the community ever complained about that

conduct in Coach Kennedy's eight years of Coaching at [Bremerton High School].[1]

If you remember, a *compliment* from a rival football coach was what started this whole thing! The complaint continued:

> But BSD was not satisfied with Coach Kennedy's full "compli[ance].". . . Instead of abiding by its written policies . . . BSD has changed the rules. In a sweeping new directive, BSD purported to prohibit on-duty school employees from engaging in any and all *"demonstrative religious activity"* that is "readily observable to . . . students and the attending public.". . . BSD's policy would prohibit all on-duty school employees, while in view of any student or member of the community, from making the sign of the cross, praying towards Mecca, or wearing a yarmulke, headscarf or a cross. After all, each of those actions is "demonstrative" religious expression and would be interpreted as such. BSD's actions violate Coach Kennedy's First Amendment rights to free speech and free exercise, as well as his rights under Title VII of the Civil Rights Act of 1965, which prohibits discrimination on the basis of religion.[2]

In case you didn't know, the Ninth Circuit is one of the most liberal appellate courts in the country. It is also the biggest and most powerful, covering the entire West Coast plus Alaska and Hawaii. Because of its track record, we knew going in that it would uphold

---

1 Complaint at 2, *Kennedy v. Bremerton Sch. Dist.* (No. 3:16-cv-05694) (W.D. Wash. 2016), https://firstliberty.org/wp-content/uploads/2016/08/Filed-Complaint. pdf.

2 Ibid., 2–3.

the district court judge's ruling. It didn't help that two of the three judges on the panel that would review my case had been Obama appointees—and the other one, appointed by George W. Bush, was a former school district attorney. That seemed like a huge conflict of interest to me.

Sure enough, the panel upheld the district court ruling, but then added a whole bunch of stuff about how they interpreted my prayer. Judge Milan D. Smith Jr. wrote:

> The context [of Kennedy's prayer] would bolster the perception that the District was endorsing religion. An objective observer would know that Kennedy had access to the field only by virtue of his position as a coach, that a Satanist group had been denied such access, and that Kennedy insists on demonstratively praying only while in view of students and spectators. . . . The relevant history would add to the perception that the District encourages prayer. An objective observer would know that during the previous eight years, Kennedy led and participated in locker-room prayers, regularly prayed on the fifty-yard line, and eventually led a larger spiritual exercise at midfield after each game. BSD states that it was not aware of this conduct until 2015, but if Kennedy were to resume his practice of praying at midfield, an objective student could reasonably infer that the District was ratifying the religious exercises that Kennedy had previously conducted. This inference would follow because the District would be acquiescing to Kennedy's conduct knowing full well that the players prayed only when Kennedy elected to do so, and that the previous practice started as an individual prayer but evolved into an orchestrated session of faith. . . . Kennedy might not have

"*intentionally* involved students in his on-duty religious activities," (emphasis added) but I have no reason to believe that the pressure emanating from his position of authority would dissipate.[3]

The irony is that a few pages later, the judge wrote, "It is worth pausing to remember that the Establishment Clause is designed to *advance* and *protect* religious liberty, not to injure those who have religious faith. Which part of any of that sounds like it's *advancing* religious liberty?"[4]

My attorneys were really fired up about the Ninth Circuit's addendum. The court was setting a dangerous precedent by stating that anyone working for the government who made an outward display of faith or religious affiliation could be terminated from their job—anything from wearing a cross necklace if you were Christian, making the sign of the cross if you were Catholic, wearing a hijab or bowing toward Mecca if you were Muslim, or sporting a yarmulke if you were Jewish.

I had a problem with that. My attorneys had a problem with that. And most Americans should have a problem with that, because it is a direct violation of our First Amendment right set forth by the Establishment and Free Exercise Clause.[5] (You learn these things when you spend nine years of your life in a lawsuit).

---

3 *Kennedy v. Bremerton Sch. Dist.*, No. 16-35801 (D.C. No. 3:16-cv-05694-RBL), 42–44 (9th Cir. June 12, 2017), https://cdn.ca9.uscourts.gov/datastore/opinions/2017/08/23/16-35801.pdf.

4 Ibid., 48.

5 "First Amendment: Congress shall make no law respecting an establishment of religion, or prohibiting the free exercise thereof; or abridging the freedom of speech, or of the press; or the right of the people peaceably to assemble, and to petition the Government for a redress of grievances. . . . The two provisions work together to ensure government neutrality towards religion: the Establishment Clause prohibits a fusion of governmental and religious functions or official governmental support

Though I never intended to become the poster boy for prayer or religious liberty, how could I not step up to defend the very constitutional rights I had joined the military to protect, which were now being stripped away from me and every other American? What was fair about that? When I was deposed after the Supreme Court kicked my case back down to the lower courts to go through discovery, the school district's attorney sarcastically jabbed, "You seem to know so much about the Constitution, what makes you an expert?"

I told him, "I'm not. I just spent twenty years defending it for buttcracks like you."[6] We had to take a break for a few minutes because I was so fired up.

Meanwhile, as my attorneys were trying to keep me in front of the media to ensure interest in my case remained high, Denise was suffering because she still worked for the school district. While I was on my national press tour, she was left to pick up the pieces I'd left behind, getting endless calls and emails from people both praising and bashing me. It was hard for her not to take it all personally. Once people discovered we were married, they really targeted her. A guy once told her that the school district should have fired her, too, for not controlling me. The hate mail, death threats, and endless emails crashed the system on more than one occasion.

As head of human resources, she also attended all the major school board and district meetings. Once my case became the number one topic of discussion, Denise was often asked to leave because of

---

for the tenets of one or of all orthodoxies, while the Free Exercise Clause protects the right of every person to freely choose his own course of religious observance free of any compulsion from the state. The two clauses, however, operate in distinct ways, and forbid two quite different kinds of governmental encroachment upon religious freedom." "Amdt. 1.5: Relationship between Establishment and Free Exercise Clauses," Constitution Annotated, Congress.gov, https://constitution. congress.gov/browse/essay/amdt1-5/ALDE_00000039.

6 I didn't really call him a buttcrack. I called him something else, but you get the idea.

the conflict of interest. That killed her. She felt ostracized from her coworkers and friends for the first several months of the case.

I could see the situation taking its toll on Denise. She would tell me that she often felt like an island floating all by herself with nobody to turn to or confide in. As things became more contentious, Denise would often come home crying from work, absolutely inconsolable. People would call her on a daily basis to scream at her and curse her out about her religious-fanatic husband messing everything up. The school had to hire round-the-clock security to monitor incoming messages and packages because someone once tried to send a bomb to it. Emails were constantly going out warning all Bremerton faculty, coaches, and staff not to speak to members of the media about the case. One day, a woman dressed in a full witch costume walked into one of the district meetings and began ranting and raving about me. Another time, members of the Seattle Atheist Group turned up and blasted me in front of my wife, and she had to remain neutral and professional even though it was eating her up inside.

At the district court, Denise had to sit across the aisle from all the people she worked with—the superintendent, her bosses, her coworkers, and her friends. None of them would look at her or speak with her. She was mad at me, she was mad at God, and she was mad at the district. She felt very cut off and alone as a result of being placed in the middle of *my* fight. She would go through times of severe anxiety and deep depression, just wanting it all to be over, but I couldn't let it drop. I knew without a shadow of a doubt that God was calling me to fight this battle. I just couldn't explain it in a way that made sense to her.

It ripped my heart out to see her come home from work in tears, day after day. She began to pull away from me and isolate herself. Every time I tried to help fix things, I seemed to only make it worse.

We argued all the time about why I wouldn't just pray in private somewhere else. She didn't understand that I had made a solemn promise to God, and that I took that vow seriously. She thought I was acting in my Marine stubbornness to make a point about my freedoms being stripped away from me—and to a degree, I was—but I was more concerned about breaking the promise I had made to God after her stroke: I had told Him that if He would save my marriage to Denise, I would do anything He asked of me. This was what He seemed to be asking me to do. If I broke that vow to Him because of a little media dust-up and a few death threats, what kind of man would that make me? I didn't understand why the very thing I had asked God to save was now in jeopardy, but I could not live with myself as the leader of my family if I broke my promise simply because things were a bit difficult.

I was determined to fight to the bitter end, just as I had been trained to do. My whole life, I had been fighting, but this was the first fight that actually meant something important. This wasn't just about me. It was about the rights of all religiously affiliated Americans. That was something worth fighting for!

It frustrated me that I couldn't seem to communicate this in a way that made sense to Denise. She would ask me why I couldn't just stop, and I would try to tell her that it was the principle of the matter. God didn't need someone to stick up for Him, but Americans did. I was fighting for them. Nobody should have to choose between their job and their faith. It was a no-brainer to me. I must have tried to tell her a hundred different ways why I felt I had been called for this particular fight, but it was like there was this impenetrable wall between us that prevented us from really hearing each other's hearts.

As the months went on, we became like strangers coexisting in the same house. I felt like a failure as a husband, as a father, as a coach, and as a man. I was hurting everybody I loved when my whole life I had tried to protect them. I would pray constantly, "Why, God, why? Please, You have to fix this! I don't know how to get through to Denise." I watched her slip into a deep depression with nobody to turn to . . . not even me. I couldn't ask her about her day because inevitably part of her day had been about my case. And she didn't want to ask me about mine because I was the one causing her this pain at work. So we would retreat to our separate corners of the house, not speaking.

Things finally reached the breaking point. We had just had another argument where I tried for the umpteenth time to make Denise understand why I was doing what I was doing, but I couldn't seem to find the right words. She was bawling her eyes out, and I couldn't live with the fact that I was putting the love of my life through this emotional turmoil any longer. I felt it would be best to remove myself from the situation so I wasn't hurting her day after day.

I had no plans other than to get in my truck and leave. I hadn't packed a bag; I had no idea where I was going to stay. I just knew I had to get out of our house and hopefully give Denise time to heal away from me.

As I walked down the stairs, I got a notification on my phone. When I saw it was a text from the Kendrick brothers, my legs gave out and I fell down the hardwood steps. As I grabbed for the banister, it broke and I collapsed. I couldn't breathe for a moment, and was trying not to lose it when I saw they had sent a video message. The Kendrick brothers, who had written and produced several hit movies, including *Facing the Giants*—the movie that had gotten me into all this—had sent *me* a video. I pushed play, and as I watched their video, I began sobbing.

Denise came running to find me collapsed on the stairs with tears streaming down my face. She asked what was wrong, but I could not talk because I was so choked up. She asked if she needed to call an ambulance, wondering if maybe I'd had a heart attack or stroke. All I could do was hand her my phone and motion to her to play the video I'd just watched.

She took my phone and sat down beside me.

"Hello, I'm Alex Kendrick, and I'm standing on the fifty-yard-line of the football field where we shot the movie *Facing the Giants* about a decade ago," the video began. "The newest movie . . . *War Room* . . . is on the power of prayer and the necessity of prayer in our lives. Sometimes you have to fight in prayer. We need it for our community, we need it for our marriages and churches, and certainly our nation.

"I just read an article about a coach named Joe Kennedy. He is located in the state of Washington at Bremerton High School. He's a twenty-year veteran from the military and has been a coach there for numerous years. Since 2008, he was inspired by . . . *Facing the Giants* to begin praying after ballgames with his team[7]. . . . After doing this all these years, it's a little odd that now the school district is investigating him for praying—even though it's voluntary for the students to come pray with him after games, and sometimes before games—and they're demanding that he stop praying.

"There is a chance that either this coming Friday night or in the near future that he could lose his job for praying. . . . So I'm encouraging everyone to pray for him and with him, and I just want to say, Coach Joe Kennedy, I am proud of you. I'm proud to stand with you and pray for you, and while I hope it never happens, I am proud to be persecuted for my faith if it happens because Jesus Christ is the most important thing in my life. So you are making a stand. You're not running for the tall grass, you're saying, 'I'm going to pray no matter what.' This is not to spit in the face of anybody, but to exercise our freedom of faith, our freedom in this country, and it's within our

---

7 Correction, I was never inspired to pray *with* my team. My team took it upon themselves to pray with *me*.

constitutional right to do so. So I encourage you to go stand with him. If you're in the region, go to the games on Friday night and stand with Joe Kennedy, the coach at Bremerton High School. I thank you for watching this video, and Coach, we're proud of you, we stand with you. May God bless you."[8]

As Denise and I sat there together, bawling our eyes out, it was like a switch flipped, and whatever had been blocking our ability to communicate came tumbling down. She finally understood what I'd been trying to tell her, and the love flowed back between us. In that moment, just as in the moment when I told God that I was going to fully surrender to Him if He would save my marriage, He once again fixed everything. It was almost as if He wanted to see if I would hold up my end of the bargain and put Him first, even if it meant risking the one thing I had asked Him to save. It was like Abraham and Isaac—I had to be willing to put the thing I loved most in this world on the altar, and after I did, God restored it to me.

From that moment on, Denise stood by my side as the most devoted and faithful supporter and told me she was proud of me. I know it couldn't have been easy since she still had to work at the school district, but God had sent that video at exactly the right moment and saved our marriage once again. Coincidence?

The fact that my case went to the Supreme Court and was given a second chance to go through the judicial system reinforced to me that this fight was worth for the effort. Four of the justices—Samuel Alito, Clarence Thomas, Neil Gorsuch, and Brett Kavanaugh—said as much when the Court denied our first petition and asked for more information to be presented later.

---

8 First Liberty Institute, "The Kendrick Brothers Support Coach Joe Kennedy," YouTube, October 16, 2015, https://www.youtube.com/watch?v=EuoJow8SaB4.

Unfortunately, the District Court's brief, informal oral decision did not make any clear finding about what petitioner was likely to be able to prove. . . . The decision of the Ninth Circuit was even more imprecise on this critical point. Instead of attempting to pinpoint what the petitioner was likely able to prove regarding the reason or reasons for his loss of employment, the Ninth Circuit recounted all of petitioner's prayer-related activities over the course of several years, including conduct in which he engaged as a private citizen, such as praying in the stands as a fan after he was suspended from his duties. . . . We generally do not grant such review to decide highly fact-specific questions. Here, although petitioner's free speech claim may ultimately implicate important constitutional issues, we cannot reach those issues until the factual question of the likely reason for the school district's conduct is resolved.[9]

The Supreme Court recognized the lower courts' errors and was going to give us another shot. The opinion concluded:

What is perhaps most troubling about the Ninth Circuit's opinion is language that can be understood to mean that a coach's duty to serve as a good role model requires [him] to refrain from any manifestation of religious faith—even when the coach is plainly not on duty. I hope that this is not the message that the Ninth Circuit meant to convey, but its opinion can certainly be read that way.[10]

---

9 *Kennedy v. Bremerton Sch. Dist.*, 586 U.S. ___ (2019), https://firstliberty.org/wp-content/uploads/2019/01/Kennedy-Cert-Deny-Statement.pdf, 3–4.
10 Ibid., 5.

The initial feeling of dejection over being denied galvanized me and my legal team to be even more thorough during round two.

The first time, we applied for a preliminary injunction in hopes of quickly getting me back on the field. This time, we went through the painful process of discovery, which included hours of depositions from everybody involved with the case. All the coaches and members of the school district that had been involved had to be deposed.

The only person I was sorry to see put on the stand was Aaron, the superintendent. I loved that guy. I still do. I had no hard feelings toward him through any of this. He was doing what his job called him to do and what his lawyers were advising him to do. It was important to me to provide him moral support at his deposition because I knew it was going to be ugly.

Aaron's deposition lasted almost eight hours. I ran into him at the courthouse snack shack before it started, and I gave him a big hug, apologizing profusely.

"Hey," he said, "we said we weren't going to take this personally, right?"

"I know, but it still makes me sick that you have to go through this."

He was so gracious. "It sucks," he agreed, "but it'll be alright."

Being deposed is like having a colonoscopy without anesthetic. Those lawyers are all up in your personal business. It is contentious, designed to trip you up. They don't really want to know the facts. They want to frame the facts to suit their agenda. And they were brutal to Aaron. He could not point out that his lawyers had been telling him what to do every step of the way because ultimately, he was the one who had to sign off on everything.

Afterward, I went over and hugged him again in front of all our lawyers and told him, "Aaron, you did so good, man. That was brutal. That had to be the worst thing ever, but you were awesome."

He hugged me back, and I said, "When this is all over, we're going to go get tore up."

I laughed. "Heck yeah, we are."

I wanted Aaron to attend my deposition too, but we were not allowed to have any contact with each other. So I asked Denise to tell him when it was taking place and let him know it would mean everything to me if he came. She did, but told me not to get my hopes up because he might not be able to take a whole day off from work to go to Seattle, but I prayed that God would work it out.

When I showed up for my deposition, Aaron was there. He stayed all eight hours. It was very emotional. I got mad, I cried, I almost got into a fist fight with one of the attorneys—it would be a great scene in a movie. By the time it was over, I was exhausted physically, mentally, and emotionally. Aaron hugged me, told me how well I had done, and that he had no idea any of what had been going on behind the scenes. His attorneys had kept him in the dark about most of the case.

I thanked him over and over for coming. It meant so much to me for him to hear my side of things, straight from my mouth, without the filter of our attorneys in a courtroom. He told me he was proud of me for standing up for what I believed in.

That was the last time I saw or spoke to him. He has since been promoted and is no longer the superintendent of Bremerton School District. I will always have the utmost respect for him.

CHAPTER 11

I ~~HATE~~ LOVE LAWYERS

Lawyers are the ~~worst~~ best. I could never have done this without them. Best bunch of robots in suits you could ever meet.

In all seriousness, I had an amazing legal team at First Liberty. They are a pro bono law firm that only handles religious freedom cases—not just for Christians, but for *all* religions. They represent Muslims, Jews, Catholics, Protestants, evangelicals, Native American tribes—any group being discriminated against for their religious beliefs.

During my case, people would ask them accusatorily, "Would you be doing this case if it were a Muslim instead of a Christian?" My attorneys would say, "Heck, yes! Do you know how much easier it would have been if Coach had been Muslim?" I love that about them.

I often refer to my legal team as my "ex-wives" because of how much time we spent together over those eight seasons. Mine was their first big case, and when I met them, they were painfully serious—no sense of humor whatsoever. Meanwhile, I'm just a big kid—I did everything I could to break through that crusty lawyer exterior. I made it my personal mission to find the humanity in them and, after a while, they actually proved to be some very cool people.

If it had not been for pro bono attorneys, I never could have taken my case to court. I didn't have the money to have attorneys on retainer for eight football seasons. Who does? The whole thing ended up costing an astronomical amount. All my legal fees were paid by generous donors who support what these guys do, and thank God for that. I never had to pay a single penny.

My First Liberty team was comprised of Mike Berry, Hiram Sasser, Jeremy Dys, and Kelly Shackelford, the president and CEO. A. J. Ferate and Jeff Helsdon were my local Washington attorneys. The team was rounded out by an absolute powerhouse, Paul Clement. When my case went before the Supreme Court, Clement tied the record for presenting the most cases before it at 119. The guy he tied with is dead; Paul's only in his fifties. He's going to blow past that record before he retires. I want to give thanks and pay tribute to my incredible legal team.

MIKE BERRY

Mike Berry was the first member I met face-to-face. He is a fellow Marine, so we hit it off right away.

The best way I can describe him is as a little Napoleon Bonaparte. He walks into the room with boundless energy, like, "Hi! I'm Mike! I have a six-pack! I run marathons and do triathlons! Look how fast I can run!" I was like that when I was a little kid because I was so small. Whereas I eventually grew, Mike did not. (To paraphrase Carly Simon, he's so vain he probably thinks this book is about him.)

In all honesty, I love Mike. He's a great guy, but when we first met, he was so serious and *always* on his phone. He could not sit still without his phone in his hands, working on something. Meanwhile, because I'm completely ADD/ADHD, I was always into something, and Mike would act like my parent, "Kennedy, don't do that. Kennedy, you can't say that on TV." I used to rib him because I knew it would get a rise out of him. Plus, because Mike was an officer whereas I was an enlisted guy, he had a superiority complex that drove me nuts, but we had some of the best times together.

I'll never forget the first time I met Mike. It was at a 5k or 10k race. He flew up from Dallas, and I told him I had a race the next morning. Mike, being a devout runner, volunteered to meet me at the starting line. At the time, my buddy Pappy—who is not the fastest runner on the planet—was running with me. Mike was about to jump out of his skin. He tried to run with me and Pappy for maybe the first mile before he started complaining that it was physically paining him to run so slowly. I wasn't going to leave Pappy, so I told Mike to just go on and run the race, and we would circle up at the finish line. He took off.

About halfway into the course, there was a bridge that was full of hornets. Mike, being one of the first guys to run across it, upset the hornets' nest, and they started swarming—hundreds of them. By the time we got to the bridge, they were all fired up and stinging everybody. I was trying to help swat the hornets away from me and Pappy and some of the other runners. We ended up getting stung dozens of times. One poor girl, who was wearing a tutu, got stung so many times, they had to rush her to the ER. By the time I got to the finish line, I was swelling up with giant welts from the stings. Meanwhile, Mike was chilling, bragging about his race time.

Mike loves to remember the story of when he came to Seattle to do the first round of press interviews with me. We met in the lobby of a downtown hotel near the studio and had a little bit of time to kill. Mike was getting a lot of calls, so he handed me the remote control to the lobby TV and walked away to a quiet corner. When he returned, I was watching *Tom & Jerry* and eating a bowl of Lucky Charms. Mike walked up with a smirk on his face, and said, "Cartoons, eh?"

"Oh, yeah, I love this episode," I said in all seriousness. He looked at me funny. To this day, he tells people that I was watching that cartoon with as much seriousness as if I had been reviewing game tape. (What can I say? I love cartoons.) He tries to psychobabble it and tell me I like cartoons because I wasn't allowed to watch them in my childhood. He tells me I was stunted as a kid.

"Okay, Mom," I always reply because I know he hates it.

Another time, Mike took me to a Vietnamese pho place. I had never even heard of pho, and he went on and on about how it was God's gift to food. While I hate to admit that he is right—pho is amazing—I go out of my way to mispronounce it because I know it drives him crazy. He always corrects me.

"It's pronounced 'fuh,'" he chides.

"That's some good 'foe,'" I reply, ignoring him.

One of the coolest experiences I ever had with Mike was at a veteran's event in Washington, D.C., where Donald Trump was speaking. First Liberty had been invited because they were representing a Navy chaplain in another case. Because I was a brand-new client and they had an extra ticket, Mike invited me to go. This was before Trump was elected, so I was blown away just to be in the room with a presidential candidate. Trump gets a bad reputation for a lot of what he did, but at this event, he really opened up and shared what he truly believed. Mike and the Navy chaplain were seated at one of the tables in front of me. I was standing in the very back where all the cameras were. Some of the most prominent generals and admirals from all the branches of the Armed Services were invited.

We listened to Trump speak and saw that he was really fired up about the troops and religious liberty. As he was talking from the podium, he started to tell a story about a football coach from Washington who was fired for praying. Mike turned around and looked at me mouthing, "That's you! He's talking about you!" I couldn't believe it. Then, a guy standing next to me that I had met in the lobby earlier started shouting, "Excuse me, Mr. Trump. The coach is here!" Trump put his hand over his eyes to try to find me in the bright lights, and asked me to tell my story. It was crazy, because I was in the very, very back of the room—I wasn't even supposed to have been there! It was a last-minute thing—and yet it was like the parting of the Red Sea, the way every head turned on either side of the center aisle to look back at me. I had to shout so Trump could hear me. All the cameras positioned above my head were straining to look down at me, and the cameramen were getting frustrated. They ended up only getting audio.

After the event, Trump shook my hand and told me I had his support. He later told the press, "Coach being fired for praying is absolutely outrageous. Outrageous. Really, really sad." That became a running joke between me and Mike. We would look at one another from time to time and just go, "Outrageous!" in our best Trump imitation.

That was the first of three times I met Trump. Me, just an average Joe from middle-of-nowhere Washington, rubbing elbows with the leader of the free world. Coincidence? Whether you like him or hate him, that was a one of the coolest experiences of my life, and Mike made it happen.

HIRAM SASSER

Hiram reminds me of Columbo—you know, the detective from the '80s show with the trench coat who would always go, "Just one more thing . . ." That's Hiram, except Hiram has a regulation haircut and a voice that is much higher than what you would expect from his appearance. He is a funny guy. He looks big and tough . . . and then he opens his mouth and it's like a cartoon character is speaking to you. When he gets excited, his voice gets really high and squeaky, like an exasperated Jerry Seinfeld. Whereas Mike shows no emotion, Hiram wears his on his sleeve.

Unlike me, Hiram knew the game of football inside and out. He could and should be a coach, he knows so much about the game. I invited Hiram to watch one of the games at Bremerton with me from the sidelines before I was suspended. One of our best players threw his helmet across the field after a flag on the play. None of the coaches had any tolerance for that, so the head coach yanked him out of the game.

Hiram was standing by me, and he got wound up. "COACH WHAT ARE YOU GUYS DOING?!" he squawked. "THAT'S YOUR BEST GUY!"

"Just watch," I told him.

He watched as the player stormed up and down the sideline, kicking and cursing and throwing a fit.

"Coach, you gonna go talk to him?" Hiram asked. "You gotta go talk to him. Get him back in the game!"

"Just watch," I repeated, ignoring the shenanigans on the sideline. Hiram grabbed his head in his hands and in his high-pitched Seinfeld voice, bellyached, "OH MY GOD."

He was having a fit.

"That's your star player!"

"I know."

"You're already down by a field goal!"

I didn't care. Hiram was really getting stressed out. After a few minutes, he tapped me on the shoulder and said, "Look, he's coming over to you! You gonna talk to him now?"

I ignored him.

I had picked up my player's helmet after he had thrown it, and I was holding it the whole time. He wasn't going to get it back unless he came over to me. After a minute or two, I felt him standing next to me.

"You need this?" I asked my player nonchalantly.

"Yes, Coach," he answered.

"How'd you lose it?" I asked, knowing the answer full well already.

"I lost my head, Coach."

"Did you find it?"

"Yes, Coach."

I helped him get his helmet on straight and tapped him on the head, saying, "You do that again, you're out for the rest of the game. Got it?"

"It won't happen again, Coach."

He ran back onto the field. I never had to raise my voice once. From behind me, I heard Hiram freaking out. "HOW DID YOU DO THAT? WHAT JUST HAPPENED? OH MY GOD, THAT WAS SO COOL!"

I hadn't done anything. That's just how I did my job. I waited for my guys to calm down and collect themselves, I talked to them, and we moved on. It absolutely blew Hiram's mind.

Hiram was excitable, so I messed with him all the time, especially in interviews. No one could ever predict what would come out of my mouth. Once, we had gotten some bad press, and the anchor interviewing us on TV brought it up to see how I felt about it.

I told him, "Some battles are fought face-to-face, man-to-man. I'm not used to fighting battles with words, so if the guy who wrote the article wants to fight, I'd be more than happy to meet him in the octagon."

Hiram almost lost it on the air. As soon as the cameras stopped rolling, he blurted out, "THE OCTAGON? DID YOU REALLY

JUST SAY THAT? HOLY CRAP, THE OCTAGON, OH MY
GOD." We laughed about that one for weeks. We still do.

I could always count on Hiram to be the comic relief at First
Liberty.

JEREMY DYS

Jeremy is the First Liberty guy I spent the most time with. He was
in charge of the media side of things, and we spent countless hours
traveling around the country on multiple press tours. When I was first
introduced to Jeremy, I remember thinking, *Did he just lose his best
friend?* Because he looked so depressed. I don't think I saw him smile
at all the first few months.

While many people have a stick up their butt, Jeremy had a
board—almost an entire fence—up his. I was amazed he could put
his own shoes on. He was so professional and so afraid of anything I
might say on air that he would constantly interrupt me. "Kennedy,
you can't say that on the air. Kennedy, you can't say stuff like this."
He'd tell me not to say something on the air, and I'd go, "Okay,
Mom," just like I did with Mike. He hated it just as much as Mike
did. Eventually he learned that I was going to do and say what I was
going to do and say, and he began to roll with it. As he started loos-
ening up, we became like Laurel and Hardy. Jeremy had a really goofy
side that I grew to love.

The more we did press junkets, the more we developed this rap-
port. It was the *Joe and Jeremy Show.* We just fed off each other's
energy, and we began to really have fun doing interviews. He got me
on CBS, NBC, ABC, FOX, Fox News, MSNBC, CNN, ESPN, PBS,
NPR—all those lettered organizations. One time, Jeremy reached out
to legendary football coach Bobby Bowden to ask for his support in
the case. Bowden was eager to lend it and even filed an amicus brief

for us. Fox News heard about it and wanted to interview me and Bobby on the air. Jeremy flew from Dallas to Seattle to be on the air with me.

When we sat down to do the interview, the host welcomed the three of us to the set but directed all her attention to me and Bowden. Jeremy was like a magnificent statue. He didn't get to say one word the entire interview. He had told his parents about it because he was so excited about getting to be on air with Bobby Bowden, but he didn't even get to introduce himself. To make matters worse, when she signed off, she thanked "both Joe and Bobby" for being there, even though there were clearly three of us in the shot. Jeremy sulked about that the whole drive back to the hotel. In the car, his mommy even called him to comfort him about how he had been ignored on the air. She told him, "Oh, Jeremy, I'm sure you would have said something wonderful!" I never let him live it down that his mommy had to call and console him for flying twelve hours round trip to be a magnificent statue in my interview. He was so butthurt about that. Still is.

At one event, Jeremy was mistaken as my bodyguard. Jeremy is 6'3", athletic, bald, always dressed in a tailored suit, and that particular day, he was wearing some kind of Ray-Ban-looking sunglasses. He has a very serious resting face, and he'll often stand off to the side with his arms crossed. At my first public speaking event, one lady came up and asked if he was my Secret Service Agent. I had to bite my tongue to keep from laughing, but when I looked over and saw Jeremy brooding in his sunglasses, I could see how she arrived at that conclusion.

After spending so much time flying around the country together for press interviews, fundraisers for First Liberty, and other keynote speaking engagements, I remember one week was especially tough, with the long hours during the trial. On our way to the airport after an event, I looked over at Jeremy and asked him, "Hey, are we friends?"

He looked at me, a little surprised and said, "Yeah, Coach. I think we're friends."

"No, are we like *really* friends?"

He thought about it a moment before answering, "Well, I'm your lawyer, so there's that relationship, but yeah, I think we're friends."

For some reason, I still wasn't satisfied, so I kept pressing. "No, but are we *actual* friends?"

"Yeah, Coach," Jeremy repeated, "We're friends. Anyone who spends the amount of time together that we have and has shared the experiences we've shared . . . we're friends."

I could tell that he sincerely meant it. I appreciated that. It was a pretty sappy but poignant moment for both of us. Of all my First Liberty "wives," Jeremy was my favorite. He made me a better person in the same way a good wife makes a better man out of her husband. He's one of my best friends. I would love to have him do interviews with me the rest of my life.

KELLY SHACKELFORD

"Kerry" is my favorite robot. He's just all business, all the time. He's a brilliant lawyer, and he helped build First Liberty from the ground up, but he's the only one I could not get to crack. I call him "Kerry" because when we went on Bill O'Reilly's show, O'Reilly couldn't remember his name correctly and kept calling him "Kerry Shackelford." It just kinda stuck from then on.

O'Reilly's staff told me he always had to have the last word, and he loved to interrupt his guests or try to provoke them with his questions and then tear their responses apart, especially if their views differed from his own. Being me, I decided to have some fun with that information.

They escorted me and Kelly onto set. Our host didn't even acknowledge we were there as the crew checked our mics for the segment. He was deep into his preparations—no hellos, no handshakes.

"So, Coach," O'Reilly said as the taping began, "You worked for Bremerton High School?"

"Yes."

He waited for me to continue. I didn't.

"And you were fired for praying on the fifty-yard-line?"

"Yes, I was."

In my peripheral vision, I could see Kelly getting fidgety. I usually love to talk. It's hard to get me to shut up. I'm not afraid of talking to anybody, but I was giving O'Reilly the bare minimum. I think it started to rattle him a bit.

"Were you trying to proselytize or convert your players to your religion?" he asked. I could tell he really wanted me to take the bait. I wasn't about to.

"Oh God no, I would never do that."

"So basically, you were going out there giving a prayer and being thankful for what happened?"

"That's right."

After a pause, he turned to Kelly, "So Kerry, what does this mean from a legal standpoint?"

I was trying hard not to laugh as Kelly launched into his spiel after O'Reilly had just called him "Kerry." Every now and again, he would try to direct a question at me, and I'd give him another one- or two-word response. Then he'd turn right back to "Kerry."

After the interview was over, we took our mic packs off, and O'Reilly looked over at me and said, "Coach, I'm going to follow up with you."

"Thanks man," I said, "I appreciate that."

His assistants were eager to rush us off the set so O'Reilly could prep for the next segment, but I walked up to his desk and extended my hand to him. Out of the corner of my eye, I could see his staffers waving me off with their arms like a 747 on the taxiway. They looked terrified that I had approached O'Reilly.

I said, "Bill, I just wanted to tell you, that was a really cool experience."

He looked up at me with an expression that said, *Who the F has the cojones to interrupt me right now?* When he saw it was me, he stood up from his desk slowly. Now let me tell you, O'Reilly is a really tall guy. He has to be 6'5". He just seemed to get bigger and bigger and bigger as he stood up to shake my hand.

"Coach," he said, "I really do wish you well, and I want you to keep me involved in your case."

"I absolutely will," I answered, and then walked out so they could start the next segment.

When we got back to the green room, the assistants were freaking out. Apparently, there are rules to appearing on *O'Reilly*, the first being that you never, ever interrupt him between segments like I just had, but we parted with a great deal of mutual respect. That was one of my favorite interview experiences.

The second time I met Trump, Kelly was with me. We were invited to the Oval Office, after he became President, to watch him sign an executive order into law regarding religious liberties. The Oval Office is much smaller than it appears on TV. Before the president came in, I got to sit behind his desk. I was like a kid in a candy shop, touching everything, and Kelly was fussing at me to stop. I tried to open all the drawers of the Resolute Desk—they were all locked—so I picked up all the challenge coins. I even picked up the phone on his desk and held it to my ear. I thought it was a prop phone, so I was shocked when I heard someone on the other line go, "Yes, sir, can I help you?"

"Uhhh, sorry, wrong number," I said, and hung up. I'm pretty sure Kelly wanted to murder me right then and there. He was so embarrassed. I so badly wanted to pull a *House of Cards* and tear a tassel off the presidential flag, but the Secret Service was watching us like hawks. I was one of maybe twenty or thirty other people there, representing different religious liberty cases, but when the president walked in and shook my hand, he went "Hey, Coach Kennedy. Good to see you, man."

You could have knocked me over with a feather. The president of the United States remembered me? He went on to introduce me to the rest of the room and all the media that were crammed in the Oval Office with their cameras: "This is Coach Kennedy from Bremerton High School. He got fired for praying and stuff. Hell of a guy. Hell of a guy, you know."

I got to stand next to Trump as he was seated at his desk, and before they let the press start asking their questions, he leaned over to me and whispered, "Watch all the jackals come to feed." The press were literally elbowing each other to get to the front of the line. Instead of asking him questions about religious liberty, which is why we were all gathered that day, they started asking him about everything else. They were all yelling over each other to try to get their questions answered. It was like there was no respect for the Office of the President whatsoever. It was so disrespectful. I wanted to tell them to shut the heck up. I seldom get offended, but I was offended by the way the media acted that day. I don't know how he or any other president deals with it.

As Kelly and I were leaving the Oval Office, I jokingly punched President Trump and said, "Sir, you've got one heck of a set of cojones on you."

He started laughing. Not just a polite laugh, but a real, unguarded, deep belly-laugh. He turned to me and punched me in the shoulder back and said, "You got a pair on you too, Coach." The Secret Service didn't think it was so funny. Kerry and I will never forget that moment as long as we live.

LISA HOLMES

As awesome as the First Liberty guys are, my favorite person at the organization is Lisa Holmes. She is an absolute angel, and she just has the most beautiful aura—or whatever you want to call it—about her. You can see the Spirit of God all over this woman. She's almost fuzzy to look at because she just shines. She was my lifesaver at First Liberty.

When you're surrounded by guys in monkey suits, it can feel very impersonal at times. They can get so hyperfocused on the case that they forget the human component. Lisa *is* the human component. She's head of client relations at First Liberty, and she would reach out to me, and especially to Denise, just to offer prayer and emotional support throughout the journey. She would send us daily devotions and take us out to lunch or dinner when we were in town and just show us the love of Christ.

After I had known her for a few months, Lisa said in her sweet little Southern accent, "You know, Coach, I actually have some ties to football."

"Awwww, were you a cheerleader?" I asked jokingly, expecting her to say she had cheered in high school.

She said, "Yeah, I was a cheerleader for the Dallas Cowboys."

"Shut the heck up!" I said. "Seriously?"

She kinda blushed and nodded.

"What years?"

"Nineteen seventy-seven to seventy-eight," she said.

"Lisa!" I exclaimed, "I had a poster of you on my wall as a kid. That was the year Dallas played Denver in the Super Bowl! I watched every game that season, and I had a poster of the Dallas Cheerleaders hanging on my bedroom wall."

Coincidence, right?

I embarrass the crap out of her about it every chance I get. I think it's the coolest. Denise and I love Lisa to death.

A. J. FERATE

A. J. was a Bremerton football alum who moved to Oklahoma to practice law. When A. J. called me, he was so down to earth. He didn't act like a lawyer. He would come to the football games to support me—giving up time from his own practice and family to fly to Bremerton to be with me. We would go on long runs together and talk about anything and everything. He would take the time to explain all the complicated legal concepts of the case in a way that I could actually understand.

At one of the last games I coached before I was suspended—the game all the press and protesters attended—A. J. was responsible for corralling me off the field for a post-game press conference. I was fired up and ready to go off on the media, but as we were walking off the field, I felt a tap on my shoulder. I turned around and saw Ray, one of the counselors from the youth ranch where I had lived as a kid, standing there with the same old sly grin he always wore. I hadn't seen him since I'd left the ranch. In that moment, all the cockiness and bravado that I was ready to take into the press conference melted away. Without ever saying a word, Ray grabbed me into a big bear hug, and I broke down crying as we just hugged each other for what seemed like forever. When he finally let go, he put his arm on my shoulder and patted me before walking away. We didn't speak at all that day, but God used him to completely change my demeanor for that press conference. I walked into it still teary-eyed and humbled. Coincidence?

I later found out that God had told Ray to drive six hours to that Bremerton game to just give me a hug. I know A. J. was grateful that he had obeyed, because he was concerned that I was going to say something stupid that day on camera.

JEFF HELSDON

Jeff was brought onto my team because the school district attorneys wouldn't even talk to my First Liberty attorneys because they were not barred in the State of Washington. It was total BS, but they told First Liberty we needed a local representative. I don't know how they found Jeff or how he found us, but God knew he would be the perfect guy for the job.

The first time I met Jeff, he went into a forty-five-minute dissertation about Doberman pinschers. Now, I love dogs—I have four—but he went into such minute details about the breed that I wanted to pull my eyes out and stuff them into my ears. I thought for sure I had just met the most boring man in America. It didn't help that he looks just like Winston Churchill. (To this day, I'll text him pictures of Churchill just to bug him.) After our first meeting, I told Mike Berry, "Please don't ever put me in a room with Jeff ever, ever again." I didn't think I could take it. But somehow, Jeff became my best friend in the whole world.

He never acted like a typical lawyer. When he represented me in district court the first time, he had to grab my arm to keep me from punching a guy for calling out my wife in the courtroom. He sat beside me and, in that moment, was my friend, not my attorney. He somehow always knew when I needed him to be a friend and not a lawyer, and I appreciated that. He told me one day, "I want to be your friend, and I want to be the guy sitting beside you going through Arlington National Cemetery when we get old, drinking and laughing about all the stupid things we did." I told him, "Brother, that's exactly what I need." He could turn the lawyer thing on and off like a switch. One moment he would be Lawyer Jeff, and at the drop of a hat he would be my best friend.

I got to know his wife, Cheri, and they would go out with me and Denise at least once a month. They were both major foodies, so we would eat great food, drink, and talk about anything not related to the case. We still do this.

When we finally went to the Supreme Court, Jeff badly wanted to get one of those feather quills they put out for the two attorneys at the head table. That was his big thing. He wanted that pen *badly*. Of course, COVID ruined everything, so he had to listen to the trial with me down the block in the First Liberty conference room, but I asked Paul Clement—the attorney who presented my case to the Supreme Court—to grab one of those pens for me. He ended up grabbing two. I put one in a shadow box with a bunch of pictures of me and Jeff throughout the years to give to him.

PAUL CLEMENT

Paul was only a member of my legal team for the last year. He is a former Solicitor General of the United States. He has tried more than a hundred cases before the Supreme Court and is well known and respected by all of the justices. I was blown away when he offered to take my case pro bono.

I didn't spend a lot of time with Paul, but in what little time we did spend together, I was amazed by how smart and eloquent he was. The night before we went to the Supreme Court, he and his wife went to dinner with me and Denise. Paul told me that his wife never gets very interested in any of his cases, but when she heard that he had been asked to represent me, she told him, "You better take this one."

She would consistently ask for updates on what was going on with my case, and she wanted to have dinner with me and Denise just to meet us and show her support.

Paul's team spent thousands of hours going through all the depositions to prepare for our case. I spent a lot of time on the phone or over Zoom with them helping provide information for all the documents they had to prepare. They were the most dedicated team, and when Paul walked into the Supreme Court to present my case, he made the opposing counsel look like amateurs. He is just a consummate professional and a stand-up guy. I'm forever grateful that he argued my case and convinced six of the nine justices to side with me.

I owe Paul, Jeff, A. J., and all of my First Liberty "wives" everything. We won the case that counted.

CHAPTER 12

ADOPTED AT 47

For a long time, I blamed my adoptive parents for everything. All that hate kept me warm at night. It was a driving force. But after Denise's stroke, when I recommitted my life to God and began developing a relationship with Him, all that hate went away. I knew I needed to make amends for being such a bad kid, so I called them up and apologized.

Family had never been super important to me, but I was about to end up with more family than I knew what to do with.

When my older sister turned eighteen, her biological mom called her and asked if they could meet. So when I turned eighteen, I expected my biological mom to do the same—but that didn't happen. Once Google came along, I would occasionally do a search to see if I could find my biological mom, but it was like trying to find a needle in a haystack—heck, it was more like trying to find a needle in the middle of the ocean. Where do you even begin?

I asked a buddy who worked at the hospital where I was born to do some digging. For a long time, my records were sealed and I couldn't access them. Then, the state changed the law so that if you had been adopted, you could file some special forms and they would release your records to you.

My son, Jacob, asked me to do that. I didn't have any objections to finding my birth mom, but I was busy with the case and didn't have time to fill out a bunch of new legal forms. Jacob told me he would print out all the paperwork and fill it out so all I had to do was look it over and sign it. He brought it to the house one day, and we mailed it in. About a month later, I received a package from Washington State. I was praying it wasn't jury duty or a speeding ticket, but when I opened it, I saw it was my birth certificate. I immediately closed the package and yelled, "Denise! Come here!" I didn't want to open it by myself.

"What does it say?" she asked.

"I don't know. You read it," I said, handing it to her.

She looked at it and told me I was listed as Baby Doe, and it listed my birth mom's maiden name and city. I called Jacob and told him.

"What are you going to do now?" he asked.

"What do you mean, what am I going to do now? We wanted to find out who my mom was, and we found out."

"You've got to look her up!" he exclaimed. He came over, and we did a Google search for Sandy Adams. Turns out, she lived in the next town over, not even an hour away. Jacob wanted to drive out there to meet her. I was concerned that this lady was probably up in years by now, and the son she had given away suddenly showing up on her doorstep might give her a heart attack. But Jacob wouldn't wait. He got in his truck with no plan and drove to her house without even stopping to put his shoes on. He literally walked up her driveway, barefoot, and rang the doorbell.

When Sandy opened the door, he said, "Ma'am, I don't know how to tell you this, but I think you're my dad's mom."

She started tearing up, and told him she'd been waiting for this visit her entire life. She immediately saw the family resemblance in Jacob's face. She invited him in, and they talked. She wanted to know everything about me.

Jacob wanted me to meet her, but I didn't know if I wanted to open a potential can of worms by starting a relationship with Sandy. She *had* given me up for adoption, after all. There must have been a reason.

I put off meeting her for almost a year after that. Jacob would visit and talk with her frequently, and she always asked him to ask me to come meet her. Finally, I drove over by myself.

Sandy started bawling her eyes out when she saw me. We talked for a while, and she told me she had been a teenager when she got pregnant. Her fiancé had gone to Vietnam to fight, and she had a one-night stand with a friend. This was in the late '60s, and her parents were God-fearing people. Abortion was not an option, but neither was keeping me. So she put me up for adoption and never even knew if I was a boy or a girl.

As we talked, I started to feel like she was very familiar to me. Not in the familial sense—although we look so much alike, it's crazy—but it was like I knew her from somewhere else.

"What have you been doing your whole life?" I asked her.

"I work at the Puget Sound Naval Shipyard."

"Where?"

"In security."

"That's where I know you!" The light in my head finally went on. "You were the one who badged me in and did my background check when I started working at the shipyard."

I remembered it like it was yesterday. I had liked Sandy the moment I saw her at the Shipyard. I thought, *I'm gonna try to schmooze this lady,* because she was all hard-faced with attitude, like all security people tend to be. They think they're above everyone else, and she was not at all into this young punk trying to butter her up to bend the rules for him. Turns out, we worked at the same shipyard all those years, and then I found out that she lived not five minutes away from the house where I grew up with Denise and Ty. Coincidence, I'm sure.

We started hanging out more, and she introduced me to her husband, Don—the guy she had cheated on when she got pregnant with me. They ended up getting married after all. I was really nervous about meeting him because I was the bastard kid his girlfriend had while he was serving his country in Vietnam. He had every reason in the world to hate my guts. Instead, he welcomed me into the family with open arms, and we bonded over war stories. He told me that before he married Sandy, her dad sat him down and told him, "Son, you have a decision to make. You can either break up with her now, walk away, and never see her again, *or* you can marry her, love her the rest of her life, and never bring this baby up again." So he married her.

He loves to pan for gold, so we will go do that together every time I visit. It is so cool because we can sit there with our pans and not speak for long periods of time, but we're completely comfortable together.

We were panning for gold a few years later when he stopped shaking his pan and randomly asked, "How would you feel if I wanted to adopt you?"

I was shocked. *Adopt me?* I was forty-seven at the time. Could I even *be* adopted? But the more I thought about it, the nicer it started to sound.

"That'd be cool," I told him. Without another word, we both went back to panning like the whole thing was no big deal.

Later he asked me again, "Were you serious about what I asked?"

"Were *you* serious?"

He said, "Yes, I've always wanted a son, and your mom gave you away . . . so, yeah. I'd like to be your dad."

That's more of a man than I could ever be. I mean, I love Denise more than anything, but if she had done what my mother did, I don't know that I could have welcomed that kid into my family and adopted him or her. But he had married her and stayed married to her for forty-eight years, and now he wanted to legally become my dad.

We found the right forms on the internet. All we had to do was get a judge to sign them, and that was it. We printed the forms out and, as we were signing them, a thought dawned on me.

"Mom?" I asked. "Are you going to adopt me, too?"

"I'm already your mom, silly," she answered.

"Yeah . . . biologically you are, but legally you're not."

That really confused her at first. When she finally understood what we were asking, she teared up. "I never thought I'd get the chance to adopt my own son," she said. "Of course I want to adopt you!"

We added her name to the paperwork, and the three of us went to the courthouse with my new forty-year-old half-sister, Shelby. Shelby thought I was the coolest thing, almost like a new puppy. She was so excited to get a new sibling. At the courthouse, the judge signed the certificates and took pictures with us. I even got a new birth certificate. I am now officially Joseph Anthony Kennedy Powell.

One day, I asked my mom about my biological father. She wasn't eager to tell me much about him except that she thought his last name was Tye, and he was from Texas. After a year or two of asking her to tell me about him, and her telling me she "couldn't remember that night," I did every possible Google search but could not find him. My friend, Norene Hermanson, who worked at the shipyard and was like

Nancy Drew, called all over Texas looking for my dad. Despite her dedication, every inquiry came up empty.

The only person by that name we couldn't contact was found on a grave marker. He was a man who had served in the Navy and died right around the time I was born; he drowned while trying to save his buddy from a frozen lake. Norene did some more digging and found his obituary. She tracked down his surviving family members, got a phone number for his brother, and gave it to me. I called and left a voicemail.

"Hi, this is Joe Kennedy. I'm in Bremerton, Washington. I served in the Marine Corps," I said. "I've got some questions about your brother, so I'd appreciate a call back. Semper Fi."

Five minutes later, I got a call.

"This is William Tye," the man said. "What can I do for you?"

"Well, sir. This might sound weird," I responded. "I understand your brother passed, but I think he might have been my dad."

Without missing a beat, the guy went, "Doesn't surprise me a bit. He was *such* a whore."

I burst out laughing. I didn't quite know how to respond to that, but we ended up talking for a while. He told me that my dad died less than a year after he had gotten out of the Navy and I had several cousins, aunts, and uncles in Texas—so I flew down to meet them. Had I not been all over the news, they probably would have thought I was some kind of gold-digging jerk, because they had zero knowledge of me whatsoever. But when they saw me for the first time, they instantly saw the family resemblance and accepted me as their relative. I was not as easily convinced and requested a DNA test, which confirmed that we were, indeed, family.

They welcomed me after that and pulled out old photo albums to show me pictures of my dad. In one of them is a picture of him with my biological mom. On the back of the photo, it said, *Me and Sandy goofing off.* Below that was another picture of the two of them with a caption that had been scratched out underneath. We passed it around trying to make out what it said. It was worn from decades of age. We put it under several different bright lights and were finally able to make it out. It said, *Sandy Adams . . . The girl who is going to have my baby in May.*

I didn't think my dad knew my mom had ever gotten pregnant, but here was solid evidence that I was part of the Tye family. We were all blown away. I took a picture of that photo and texted it to my mom. She immediately texted back, "Where did you get that?"

She was so busted.

"What happened to 'I can't remember'?" I asked her. She fudged, clearly caught red-handed. I sent her a few more pictures of the two of them together, and then she finally confessed about their relationship.

In only a few years' time, I went from having no family to finding both of my biological parents and being adopted at the age of forty-seven. Just a coincidence, right?

CHAPTER 13

IT'S A FREEDOM THING

It was really important to me, in the course of writing this book about my crazy life, to finally be able to talk about why I did what I did. I've been made out to either be a religious nutjob or some sort of Christian superhero when I'm just me. I'm not perfect. In fact, I'll be the first to tell you that I'm far from it. My relationship with God has been a convoluted journey from Catholicism to agnosticism to whatever I am now. People ask me, "Oh, what denomination do you belong to?" I don't know.

I have a personal relationship with God, and that's that. I'm a simple guy. I like to look at things in their stripped down, barest essence. For me, that means I have three loves: my love of God, my love of my wife, and my love of my country. I would defend or take a bullet for any of them, and in both the literal and figurative sense, I have.

My adoptive parents were hardcore Catholics. We went to Mass every Sunday when I was growing up. They had all the right boxes checked in that arena, but I was always questioning everything, including whatever I learned in Sunday school. I didn't want to be ornery; I just wanted to understand. The more I asked why, the more frustrated I got when people would give me shallow, churchy answers or would just tell me to stop asking questions altogether. How was I supposed to understand what I should believe in if no one could explain it to me?

The older I got, the more that orneriness did eventually turn into rebellion. It wasn't until I went off to the boys' home the first time that I finally gave God a try. I fought it for a good six to eight months, but Ray finally told me, "If you don't like it, you can always quit." That made sense! When I asked him questions, he would do his best to explain every single thing and back it up with Scripture. He encouraged my questions and encouraged me to question God directly and see what I heard. Once I started doing that, I actually started to hear God through so many of the "coincidences" that happened through my life. God became real during those times. It became more of a relationship, a discussion. It was personal and alive.

Looking back, I don't know how I ever doubted God, because He always seemed to answer even my most trivial prayers. When I was at the boys' home, we were out working in the fields on a 110-degree day, and I suddenly wanted some watermelon. I told God, "It would be so cool if we could get some watermelons." That day, a local grocery store donated an entire truckload of watermelons that were about to go bad. There must have been hundreds of them. It was like God was asking me, "What do I have to do to prove to you that I'm real?"

But I was always such a doubting Thomas. It was like I had an angel on one shoulder and a devil on the other, and they were always arguing. When I was at the boys' home, it was easy to believe in God because I was in that environment day in and day out, but when I went back home, and especially after I joined the Marine Corps, my environment changed and so did my relationship with God.

It was hard to be a Christian in the Marines for many reasons—one being that G-O-D stood for Good Order and Discipline. The other God was a nice story that you told somebody because you knew they were going to die. That stuck with me for a while, especially in Desert Storm. In my reality, when one of our brothers died, they went into the ground and that was it. You're born, you live, you die, you cease to exist. We would speculate and debate the existence of God, but the world seemed so cruel that it was easier to just believe in what we could see and feel. It started to sound more like a fairy tale that only good people went to Heaven and bad people burned in Hell.

That all changed when I started going back to church with Denise and surrendered everything to God at the altar in a last-ditch effort to save our marriage.

Before that, I didn't want to submit to anyone. After that, I didn't want to submit to anyone but God. Even though I liked our pastor, I would butt heads with him a lot. One day he called me out for being a goat instead of a sheep. As a Marine, I took issue with that. Sheep are stupid. I know—I used to work around them at the boys' home. They mindlessly follow. I wasn't about to be like some dumb sheep. I had a big fight with the pastor and ended up going to another church. Denise wasn't happy because she was heavily involved in our church as a youth leader, so for almost a year, we went to two different churches.

The new church I started going to was much more about redemption and love. I liked that. The messages were more centered on God and people than "the church" as a building. At that point in my spiritual growth, that's what I needed to hear. I needed a place where I could learn to have a relationship with God. Eventually, Denise came on board and started going to the new church with me.

Up until that point, I could still hear God when I talked to Him, even though I wasn't living a good Christian life, so to speak. It's hard to explain, but after I surrendered to Him, I stopped hearing that voice. It freaked me out. I liked being able to argue with that voice. I went to visit the pastor at the new church, and he told me I didn't need to hear the voice anymore because God now lived inside me. He told me that before I surrendered my life to God, the Holy Spirit would speak to me externally because I had not invited Him into my heart. After I invited Him into my heart, He no longer needed to communicate with me externally because He now lived inside me. It blew my mind. I thought that was the coolest, weirdest, smartest thing I'd ever heard in my life. Whereas I used to hear the voice, now I get more of an internal feeling. Now I can look at a person and know that something's going on with them. It's like God just gives me a feeling that I need to go up and talk to a particular person, and if I don't, I get that horrible dirty feeling just like I did that one night I didn't do my prayer on the field. I've learned to listen to that.

My theology—if that's what you want to call it—is very simple. I believe in God the Father, and I believe that He had a literal son whose name was Jesus. I mean, He's in the history books. There's tons of proof that supports His existence, His death, and His resurrection.

To me, the whole Christian walk boils down to two simple concepts: love God and love others. And guess what? I fail at those two simple things every single day. I try to do the best I can, and I pray all the time. Not big fancy prayers—just short, "Hey God, You're awesome," type prayers. Someone told me that the Bible says to pray without ceasing, and I do. I give thanks to God throughout the day, I pray for others, and I mostly pray for forgiveness every single night. I think people overcomplicate Christianity with their rules when really, we just need to be decent human beings and love each other. I live by the Universal Rule: Don't be a jerk.[1]

---

1 I actually use a more alliterative word here but, you know . . .

Some of the coolest experiences I've had regarding faith occurred while talking to people who are not even the slightest bit Christian or religious. Early on in the trial, I got a Facebook message from the cofounder and president of a Seattle atheist group. It was the largest one in the state of Washington. He was trying to condemn me for my prayer based on what he'd read in the press. After a few back-and-forth exchanges, I wrote to him and said, "Why don't we get together for a cup of coffee and let me explain to you, in person, why I'm doing what I'm doing before you make such a hard judgment of who you think I am?" Most of the time, when I did this with Facebook trolls, they would turn me down and curse me out, but this guy decided to take me up on my invitation.

We met at a local Christian-owned burger joint called Noah's Ark, close to Bremerton High School. He asked me why I insisted on praying and how it wasn't legal, and he gave me all these reasons to back up his opinion. He was a really intelligent guy, and he seemed genuinely curious, so I told him, "Dude, I was a Marine. The Constitution means something to me. This isn't about spreading my religious beliefs or converting people to my faith. This is about my right to freedom of religious expression as an American." I talked about how all the freedoms in the Constitution and the Bill of Rights should apply to every American, including me. I wasn't asking for more freedoms than anybody else; I just wanted to exercise the rights guaranteed to me as a citizen.

He cut me off and tried to redirect the conversation back to the religion aspect, but I told him that his line of questioning was irrelevant. It didn't matter where I prayed. I could be a Christian anywhere. The issue I had with the school district was that they were trying to take away my right to pray. He paused for a minute and looked at me, somewhat confused.

"So, this really isn't about forcing religion on anybody?" he asked.

"No!" I replied.

Once he finally understood that it was about protecting a constitutional freedom and not converting a bunch of impressionable kids, he suddenly got really interested. We sat there talking for over two hours. At the end of the conversation, he said, "You know who you remind me of, Coach?"

I had been compared to Daniel in the lions' den so many times throughout the case that I was silently praying to myself, *Don't say "Daniel," don't say "Daniel."*

"You remind me of the Apostle Peter," he continued.

Not being familiar with all the apostles, I asked him, "Which one is that again?"

"Peter is the one who denied Jesus," he explained. "When Jesus was arrested, before He was sent to be crucified, the Roman guards approached Peter three times to ask him if he knew Jesus. Each time, Peter denied that he knew Jesus. You did what Peter couldn't do. You had every chance to deny your faith, but you stood by it in spite of the consequences. That's pretty cool."

"That's really cool!" I exclaimed. I'd never heard it put that way before. I hadn't read that story in the Bible.

He explained that Peter was asked three times to deny Jesus, and he did. I was asked three times by the school district via their directive letters to stop praying, but I didn't. If a rooster had started crowing in the exact moment when he told me that, I'd have freaked out!

Before we parted ways, the guy told me, "I'm on your side, Coach. I'll back you with anything you need. I thought you were gonna be a religious nutjob who was out there trying to brainwash kids with the Bible, but you're nothing like that."

"Definitely not," I agreed.

We had shown up to that lunch as two people who seemed different in every possible way, yet we parted on friendly terms. I've found that most people who allowed me the chance to explain my beliefs and why I was really doing what I was doing would come around to my side and throw their support behind me. It was never a religion thing. It was always a freedom thing. It was a freedom thing that just happened to also be a religion thing.

What kind of Christian would I be, what kind of husband would I be, what kind of leader and coach would I be if I didn't lead by example? I always told my players how important principles were. I couldn't abandon mine just because things got a little tough or uncomfortable. That would have made me the biggest hypocrite.

People ask why I fought this fight, and I say it's because it needed to be done. I just happened to answer the call. Anybody else could have done it. There's nothing special about me. It was the calling that I felt God leading me to accept, and I still wrestled with that.

From the time my Facebook post went viral, I began wondering if I was doing the right thing. I hated going against the school district. The way everything unfolded made me question my motives constantly. I wondered if I had really heard God, because I just wanted to coach football. Yet, in spite of all my questioning, I undeniably felt like this was my fight in the same way I felt God's hand reach through the TV screen when I was contemplating whether or not to even start coaching. It just seemed like His hand was in this the whole time, even though I couldn't explain why or why me. I didn't want to make a big ruckus or spend nine seasons of my life in the courts, but I had made a commitment to God, and I wasn't about to go back on that promise.

That didn't mean it was easy, though. I prayed many times that God would make it all just go away. Had it been anything else, I probably would have tried to settle, but I fought for the Constitution for all Americans, and I would be darned if somebody tried to take my constitutional right away because it was inconvenient or offensive to them. It doesn't matter if you're black or white, male, female, Muslim,

Jewish, Christian, or believe in unicorns—the Constitution applies to all Americans.

Even though I'm no expert on constitutional law, when I was in the Marines, we had classes on the Constitution. We had to know what it was and what was written in it. That document is me. It's you. It's every American. It is our American card that explicitly tells us what our rights are as Americans. I was trained to fight and protect that document. That's the whole reason I fought this battle. It wasn't about Christianity or religion, and it wasn't about a political party—it was always a freedom thing for me.

When I look back, I see how my whole life prepared me for this fight. From the times I would get in trouble because I wanted to stick up for the little guy to the time I decided to give God a try and Reverend Shoals showed me that ugly tree that would survive in the harshest of circumstances; from the times that the Marine Corps broke me down, built me back up, and taught me to be a leader to the times that I passed those lessons on to my players; from the times God was real to me to the times that He wasn't and then became real once more. Everything in my life was being used by God to prepare me for this fight. Were there other, more qualified people who could have done it in my place? Absolutely. But for some reason, God seemed to pick the least likely candidate—an orphaned, unwanted, screw-up of a kid who questioned everything—to fight this one.

CHAPTER 14

SCOTUS ROUND 2

I joke about things in my life being coincidences, but I know that nothing has been. Even the way the Supreme Court kicked my case back down to the lower courts was used by God to give us time for the Court's political leanings to radically change. By the time my case made its way back, several new justices had been appointed by President Trump, and the Court was shifting back to more traditional, conservative values.

Associate Justices Gorsuch and Kavanaugh had only recently been confirmed the first time my case went before the court and were two of the four justices who wanted to hear my case again once the facts were clarified. In the meantime, President Trump also confirmed Justice Amy Coney Barrett. She, Gorsuch, and Kavanaugh all reflected conservative values, which boded well for my case. Coincidence?

In addition to the political climate changing, things had changed in our family as well. Denise resigned from her job at the school district so we could move to Florida to be close to her dad, Ron. He had been through a divorce, lost his business, and his son—Denise's brother, who had been looking after him—was murdered, all in the same week. Denise moved down immediately while I stayed behind in Bremerton for a few months to coordinate the rest of the move.

It was hard to resign from the Naval Shipyard, where I had been making a big, fat paycheck. I didn't even know how to resign initially. I called up a buddy to ask how to do it. He sent me the paperwork, and I turned it in on April 1. After a few weeks, I had had no response regarding it, so I called my boss to follow up.

"Hey, I was calling to follow up on my resignation papers," I said.

"Wait, you were serious about that?" he asked.

"Well, yeah," I said, "I'm moving out of state."

"Dude, you turned your papers in on April Fool's Day! I thought it was a joke."

"No, it's not a joke!" It was pretty funny though.

I moved down to Florida right before COVID-19 shut everything down. We were hoping to sell our house in Port Orchard, just outside Bremerton, pretty quickly. Unfortunately, COVID prevented our realtor from even showing the house for several months. Having two mortgages stank. That put us in some financial difficulties, but since there were very few places hiring during the shutdown, I got a job digging graves at the cemetery across from my neighborhood.

We bought a little house just around the corner from Ron that needed lots of repairs, so we holed up in our new little slice of sunny paradise doing fixer-upper projects while we desperately waited for our house in Washington to sell. Plus, having lived in Washington most of my life, the Florida heat and humidity took some getting used to. Denise immediately fell in love with our new home and felt like the generous dose of vitamin D was a welcome change from the constant clouds and rain she didn't even realize she had found so depressing. For me, it took much longer to come around to living in a state that has two seasons: melt your face off (also known as the tourist season) and "the off-season" which is a bipolar rotation of muggy cold and humid hot where you don't know whether to wear a jacket or a tank top from one day to the next.

During lockdown, we welcomed four dogs, two cats, and a couple chickens into our brood and enjoyed a much-needed break from the drama of Denise working at the school district and me traveling for endless media appearances related to the case. We got to spend a lot of quality time together as we waited for our Supreme Court date. I started working part-time at the Pensacola Memorial Gardens as a grave digger. It was the perfect job for that time of my life. It got my mind off the case, I got to work outside with my hands, and none of my patrons complained. Once lockdown let up, I decided to work for Tractor Supply Company, helping little old ladies haul giant bags of dog food to their car.

In the meantime, First Liberty asked Paul Clement to join my legal team and present my case before the Court. Paul's record speaks for itself. He is a brilliant speaker and had a team of the most hard-working paralegals working around the clock for the big moment. As the pandemic dragged on, we finally got our court date: April 25, 2022.

The night before the oral arguments, Denise and I attended an event where many supporters prayed for us and our attorneys. They offered words of encouragement, asked for photos and autographs, and thanked me for what I was doing. The whole thing was like an out-of-body experience, as if I was watching it from someone else's point of view. It was like I was disconnected from my own body and taking it all in.

Denise and I were shuttled into a press bus to the Supreme Court the next morning, sitting across a table from each other in giant black leather chairs looking out the window as we drove through downtown

Washington, D.C. My "other wife," Jeremy, was with us, and as we pulled to a stop, he asked me how it felt being at the Supreme Court. I told him, "I'll let you know when we get there."

He looked at me like I was stupid and said, "Look out the window."

I did and saw a giant white stone building that was pretty fancy-looking. Jeremy saw that I still wasn't putting two and two together, so he told me, "Coach, that's the Supreme Court."

I had no idea. He gave me grief about that for the longest time.

As we climbed the white marble steps with our posse of attorneys, it seemed like everyone was there: swarms of press and protestors, plus my entire legal team. Everybody was in attendance: my Washington lawyers, Devon, A. J., and Jeff; my entire First Liberty team including Mike, Hiram, Jeremy, and Kelly; and the man of the hour, Paul, and his legal partner Erin Murphy. We all stood for the hundreds of socially distanced members of the press. I took photos in my blue Bremerton polo shirt, taking a knee with a football in front of the most famous courthouse in America. I got interviewed by a guy dressed in cosplay as the anime character Akatsuki. Out of all the major news outlets lined up, this guy stood out in his long black robe with red clouds on it. I left the interview with the serious press corps that I was in the middle of to go talk to the Akatsuki guy, and I granted him an exclusive, much to my lawyer's dismay.

After we wrapped up the pre-hearing media blitz, Paul and his legal aid went into the courtroom and the rest of us walked across the street to the First Liberty's offices to listen via C-SPAN radio. As I walked away from all the protesters and press, I couldn't help but think that this whole thing was so crazy. All these people were here making all this ruckus over my thirty-second prayer. All I had wanted was a clear-cut legal answer to the question that started this whole process to begin with: do I have the constitutional right to pray on the field or not? For someone who likes to see things in black and white, it drove me nuts that the lower courts had not been able to answer that one, seemingly simple question. They had dragged in their agendas and "the political climate" instead of just telling me what the law said. I wanted a clear answer so I could go back to coaching football. Finally, I was about to get one.

Frustratingly, after eight seasons of fighting this battle, I was informed that I would not be allowed to attend my own Supreme Court hearing! I felt like this should have been illegal. Even though things had relaxed in terms of social distancing and wearing masks by this point throughout the country, the Supreme Court building would not allow anybody but the two attorneys presenting for both sides into the court room . . . oh, and all the press. It annoyed the crap out of me that the press could attend my trial, but I couldn't.

I sat with Denise and the rest of our team at a big U-shaped wooden conference table. Denise and I held hands the whole time, doing our best to listen and understand what was being said. Whenever I tried to ask questions, Jeff would shush me so he could hear. Jeremy stood in the back of the room, playing on his phone, and I drank Red Bulls like there was no tomorrow. All the caffeine didn't help the fact that my heart was already pounding out of my chest from nerves. Lisa, who was recovering from a recent hospital stay back in Plano, joined us by Zoom call. I could see her silently praying as she watched me and Denise through the camera lens while we listened to the hearing.

Paul told us that before the Supreme Court justices take the bench before each case, they say a prayer in the wings of the courtroom. It's not a long-drawn-out thing, but a short prayer followed out of a long-standing tradition. This seemed especially fitting for my case.

After the gavel was struck, Paul stood up to make his opening statement on my behalf. I was so glad to have him presenting my case and thought, had I been a judge on that panel, he'd have convinced me. He explained that my post-game prayer was doubly protected by both the Free Exercise and Free Speech clauses of the First Amendment

After his opening remarks, the justices got to ask questions not just pertaining to my exact case but to the greater ramifications a victory or loss would hold for the rest of the country. The Supreme Court has to think of the country at large, not just what is best for a single individual. It wasn't just my religious freedom at stake—it was the religious freedom of the entire United States.

The justices grilled Paul on why my prayer should be considered the act of a private individual rather than a government act. Not in an adversarial way—it was all very formal and dignified, but intense! They asked him to define why what I did was not coercion, even though the record clearly stated that it wasn't. They asked him where the lines could be drawn in terms of religious expression if, for an example, a student or teacher wanted to show their affiliation with the Nazi party. They had to go through the factual record gathered through all the hours of depositions. They examined dozens of cases that had been used as precedents and how the laws could change and those cases be overturned if the justices ruled in my favor. They questioned Paul thoroughly for almost an hour and, thanks to his diligent research and preparation, he was able to answer each question eloquently and completely. By the time they had exhausted all their questions, I was feeling pretty confident of our chances.

That confidence only grew after Bremerton's attorney stepped up for his opening remarks.

The Bremerton School District had hired Richard Katskee with Americans United for the Separation of Church and State, formerly known as Protestants and Other Americans United for Separation of Church and State. Katskee's opening remarks painted me as an attention-seeker out to coerce impressionable young kids to join my religious act. The justices grilled him just as thoroughly as they had grilled Paul—but unlike Paul, Katskee was not nearly as polished or well-prepared, in my opinion. He tried several times to argue that my prayer was disruptive and irresponsible, taking me away from my coaching responsibilities. From my layperson's perspective, the justices didn't seem to care about me and my individual responsibilities as much as they cared about something called the Lemon Test.[1]

The Lemon Test was established in the 1950s as a way to determine what is considered private speech versus what is considered public or government speech. Justice Kavanaugh seemed to be of the mind that my case rendered the Lemon Test an outdated method of determining the difference. When this came up, all my attorneys in the board room sat up at attention. I swear they all did a simultaneous double take and began asking each other, "Did he just bring up the Lemon Test?"

I didn't realize what a big deal the Lemon Test was in the legal world. Kelly Shackelford's secret life-long legal mission was to get it repealed. He didn't think it would happen during his lifetime, but suddenly Kavanaugh and several of the other justices were discussing that very thing. They then began discussing the differences between a coach's role on the field or in the locker room as opposed to his private actions between those moments. Why was it so wrong for me to take a knee rather than, say, call my wife after a football game to celebrate a win? Or why was it so wrong for me to take a knee rather

---

1 "The Supreme Court often uses the three-pronged *Lemon* test when it evaluates whether a law or governmental activity violates the establishment clause of the First Amendment. Establishment of religion cases tend to involve government aid to religion, such as aid to parochial schools, or the introduction of religious observances into the public sector, such as school prayer. The Court measures the aid or program against the prongs of the test. The *Lemon* test, considered aptly named by its critics, derives its name from the landmark decision in *Lemon v. Kurtzman* (1971)." Richard L. Pacelle Jr., "Lemon Test," The First Amendment Encyclopedia, 2009, https://www.mtsu.edu/first-amendment/article/834/lemon-test.

than making the sign of the cross? These were all private actions, even for a coach at a government-run school.

Katskee kept trying to reframe the issue of Me + Prayer = BAD, but things did not seem to be going his way.

After nearly another hour, the justices exhausted their questions with Katskee, and Paul was allowed to make his closing rebuttal. This was his moment to really knock the ball over the fence, and he did just that. He stated that there needed to be a different test for religious expression cases like mine. He reiterated that there was no evidence of coercion in the record, nor was there any evidence of me neglecting my duties as coach for the thirty seconds that I used to take a knee at the fifty-yard line. He made it clear that I had been suspended from my job for no other reason than religious discrimination. He said, "If you want to give courts and district courts—rather, school districts—guidance, the last thing you should do is replace jurisprudence that's becoming clearer and could be made clearer in this case about discrimination against religion and replace it with . . . a balancing test [that] doesn't provide guidance." He argued that it didn't matter where I chose to pray, but for the school district to tell me to reorient myself or lose my job as a result of my religious act was unconstitutional, regardless of the Lemon Test or any other precedent they examined during the hearing.

After Paul concluded his rebuttal, Chief Justice John Roberts thanked both sides and banged the gavel to close the hearing.

We rushed from the First Liberty conference room back across the street, making our way through all the crowds and protesters to reunite with Paul at the base of the courthouse steps. Not just anybody could be allowed on the steps on court days. We were allowed because ours was one of the cases being heard. As we all gathered for more pictures and interviews with the press, we thanked Paul and his team wholeheartedly for the incredible job they had done.

Denise and I flew home the next day to wait for the results, which wouldn't be announced until the end of June, after the Court had adjourned for the season. It felt like a long wait.

CHAPTER 15

WE WON THE ONE
THAT COUNTS

Around the middle of June, I flew to Dallas to the First Liberty headquarters to wait for the Supreme Court's decision on my case to be handed down. Mine wasn't the only big decision that was set to come down that month. There was also a decision on overturning *Roe v. Wade* that was going to make waves in the news. We secretly prayed that that decision would come down with enough time to go through the news cycle before mine was announced.

Our prayers were answered. The decision in the abortion case was leaked by the press ahead of its official release. It stirred up people on both sides of the issue so much that by the time the actual decision was published, they seemed to have calmed down a bit.

From then on, every day was hurry up, hurry up, wait. I would check in with the legal team each morning at 9:00 a.m. central daylight time, and we would sit around a conference table, everybody refreshing their many devices for news of my case.

Every day for a week, we waited. Denise had stayed behind in Florida, where she'd gotten a job at a florist shop (which she loved) in addition to taking care of our six animals and her father. I had booked a one-way ticket to Dallas because I had no idea when the decision would be announced. After a week of hanging in Dallas, I was eager for it to be over with so I could get home.

On Monday morning, June 27, 2022, the decision—seventy-five pages long, written by Gorsuch—came down. As my attorneys scanned the document, the room exploded into celebration: The Supreme Court had ruled in my favor, with six of the justices—Gorsuch, Barrett, Kavanaugh, Thomas, Alito, and Chief Justice John Roberts—voting "for" me, and three (Associate Justices Sonia Sotomayor, Elena Kagan, and Stephen Breyer) voting "against" me. There was high-fiving and laughing, cheering and clapping.

It lasted all of two minutes before my attorneys began dissecting the document for every ounce of information they could digest.

The summary made it unequivocally clear that I had acted within my constitutional rights when I took a knee on the fifty-yard line after each football game. The opinion stated:

> No one questions that Mr. Kennedy seeks to engage in a sincerely motivated religious exercise involving giving "thanks through prayer" briefly "on the playing field" at the conclusion of each game he coaches. The contested exercise here does not involve leading prayers with the team; the District disciplined Mr. Kennedy *only* for his decision to persist in praying quietly without his students after three games in October 2015. . . . By its own admission, the District sought to restrict Mr. Kennedy's actions at least in part because of their religious character. . . . The District explained that it could not allow an on-duty

employee to engage in *religious* conduct even though it allowed other on-duty employees to engage in personal secular conduct.[1]

Finally, somebody recognized that the school district had taken away my constitutional right to religious expression. I don't know what Gorsuch's personal faith convictions are, or if he has any, but it felt to me that God had used him to understand, articulate, and defend what I'd been trying to do for the entire nation! It was so vindicating. The opinion continued:

> When Mr. Kennedy uttered the three prayers that resulted in his suspension, he was not engaged in speech "ordinarily within the scope" of his duties as a coach. He did not speak pursuant to government policy and was not seeking to convey a government-created message. He was not instructing players, discussing strategy, encouraging better on-field performance, or engaging in any other speech the District paid him to produce as a coach. Simply put: Mr. Kennedy's prayers did not "ow[e their] existence" to Mr. Kennedy's responsibilities as a public employee. The timing and circumstances of Mr. Kennedy's prayers—during the postgame period when coaches were free to attend briefly to personal matters and students were engaged in other activities—confirms that Mr. Kennedy did not offer his prayer while acting within the scope of his duties as a coach.[2]

---

1 *Kennedy v. Bremerton Sch. Dist.*, 597 U.S. ___ (2022), https://www.supremecourt.gov/opinions/21pdf/21-418_i425.pdf, 2.

2 Ibid., 3.

That was the answer to the question I'd been seeking all along. Even though the Supreme Court clearly showed that I had won my case, it was as important to me to get the answer to my question of whether my prayer should have cost me a job that I loved.

Gorsuch reversed the Ninth Circuit's opinion, saying:

> The District, like the Ninth Circuit . . . insists Mr. Kennedy's rights to religious exercise and free speech must yield to the District's interest in avoiding an Establishment Clause violation under *Lemon* and its progeny. The *Lemon* approach called for an examination of a law's purposes, effects, and potential for entanglement with religion. In time, that approach also came to involve estimations about whether a "reasonable observer" would consider the government's challenged action as an "endorsement of religion." But—given the apparent "shortcomings" associated with *Lemon's* "ambitiou[s]," abstract, and ahistorical approach to the Establishment Clause—this Court long ago abandoned *Lemon* and its endorsement test offshoot. In place of *Lemon* and the endorsement test, this Court has instructed that the Establishment Clause must be interpreted by "reference to historical practices and understandings."[3]

When my lawyers read this and discovered that the seventy-year-old Lemon test had been reversed—and rendered officially obsolete as the test for determining religious liberty cases—they became doubly excited. Kelly Shackelford, in particular, was momentarily dumbfounded. He never thought that would happen during his lifetime. He had hoped, in his law career, to begin laying the seeds that future generations would see the Lemon Test rendered obsolete. Even though I

---

3 Ibid., 4.

didn't understand the nuances of any of that, I knew enough at that point to understand that my case suddenly had historic consequences.

Gorsuch's opinion concluded:

> There is no conflict between the constitutional commands of the First Amendment in this case. There is only the "mere shadow" of a conflict, a false choice premised on a misconstruction of the Establishment Clause. . . . Mr. Kennedy is entitled to summary judgment on his religious exercise and free speech claims.[4]

After eight years of fighting, it was over. Even though we had lost every trial along the road for the past nine seasons, we had finally won the one that counted. And we had won in an even bigger way than any of us expected. As my attorneys scoured the rest of the seventy-five-page opinion and had their happy-lawyer nerdfest, I had a few minutes to call Denise before Kelly and I were rushed into First Liberty's on-campus studio to begin interviews. Even though I had been vindicated for my prayer and embarked on a whirlwind interview marathon fueled by adrenaline and more Red Bull, by the time I got back to my hotel room late the first night, I had been smiling so much that my face physically hurt. The decision in my case was the only one announced that day, so we got all the media attention.

In my hotel room by myself, the whole thing suddenly seemed to have been anticlimactic. Don't get me wrong, it was awesome, but at the same time, Denise was in Florida and I couldn't share it with her. I just wanted to hug my wife and enjoy the fact that everything was now behind us. Instead, I had to settle for buying the only bottle of wine in my little hotel and celebrating alone because by the time I wrapped interviews around midnight, Denise was already asleep. I

---

4 Ibid., 5.

barely even got to talk to her those first few days because it was non-stop chaos.

Denise was out delivering flowers when she heard the news. She had been trying to refresh her phone all morning to see the story when it broke, but she was having difficulty with her cellular service. She found out when Lisa from First Liberty texted her to inform her of the victory. Denise told me she felt like laughing, crying, and shouting all at the same time, but she had no one to share it with.

When she returned from her delivery route, she must have had a strange look on her face, because her boss asked her if everything was okay. Denise told her boss that I had won my Supreme Court case. Everyone at her work wanted to know what was going through her mind, just as all of the media I talked to wanted to know what was going through mine. Neither of us knew how to feel. It was bizarre and surreal for both of us.

After three days of marathon interviews from 5 a.m. til 11 p.m. straight, I was burned out and ready to fly home. In those three days, we did more than eighty-three interviews. My attorneys asked me to stay another couple of days to do even more press, but I had to get home to my wife. I flew home and took Denise and her dad out for a nice steak dinner up the road from our house. It was nice return to normal. We talked about everything but the case, but every so often, I would just look over at Denise with a great big grin. She knew exactly what that meant, and she would smile back at me. We didn't have to say a single word. She just understood.

When we finally got back to the house together, I saw she had collected every newspaper she could find that mentioned the case while I'd been away. She had articles clipped from the *Wall Street Journal* and the *New York Times*. There was even an *ESPN World* article that I thought was the best of them all. As we caught up, I found myself beginning to wonder, *So what's next?*

CHAPTER 16

THE NEW NORMAL

I went back to working part-time at Tractor Supply Co. after the case as I tried to figure out the next steps. My attorneys began immediately negotiating with the Bremerton School District to plan my return to the field but—in all honesty—I didn't know if I even wanted to go back. It seemed so weird to admit that, after eight seasons of fighting to get my job back, returning to the field would undermine everything I fought for.

I had fought for my right to pray privately. It was never supposed to have been an attention-seeking event, but if I returned to Bremerton to coach, it would become exactly that. I already had news organizations asking when my first game would be because they wanted to send camera crews to film it. The people who supported me from the beginning were sending emails saying that they wanted to join me on the field for my first game back. Everybody wanted to see the return of the praying coach and witness the first prayer back on the field, and that just made me feel *oogie*.[1] I didn't want my prayer to become an even bigger media event. Then again, how could I disappoint my attorneys after all they had done for me? How could I disappoint the millions of Americans who had supported me? But in the same breath, how could I disappoint God for all He had done for me by turning it into yet another media circus—and this time, knowing that's what it would be?

Thankfully, those questions were postponed by the fact that the school district was not willing to welcome me back with open arms—not that I expected them to. However, I didn't expect them to make us go back to the district court a third time over idiotic little details about my reinstatement. Even though the Supreme Court had granted a summary judgment in my case—which meant that I had won free and clear and should be reinstated without question—the school district wanted to know what would happen if the players wanted to join me on the field for prayer, how far I needed to be from them and other people on the field, what did "praying alone" mean, and how long was a "brief prayer"?

By that point, I was getting irritated. That was what had started this crap in the first place—them trying to tell me when and where and how I could pray. The Supreme Court said I had the right to pray, and now the district was going to be nitpicky and drag things out even more? They were really being adversarial about the whole thing.

Then I started wondering if I even had another football season in me. Denise and I were established in Florida. We had family there, we had our new church family, and we had new friends. What would it look like if I were to go back to coaching? Would we move back to Washington? Would I travel back and forth? Would I go back for one game and then hand in my letter of resignation?

---

1 "Oogie" is a word I created that means filthy or creeped out, like bugs are crawling on my skin.

And, of course, there were the logistics to consider regarding the team as well. How would the players react to me barging in like some big shot after a nine-season absence? All the coaches I had worked with had retired or moved on to bigger and better things. I couldn't blame them if they didn't want me back as a coach because they had survived so long without me. Would it be selfish of me to return and disrupt the status quo of an existing team?

After spending my entire life fighting—whether it was people, wars, or legal battles—I realized I was tired. Yet at the same time, it was weird not to have an enemy to fight against or a cause to fight for. It was like I had no purpose, and I hated that feeling. It kept me up at night, wondering what the next step would be. It seemed like everybody else had plans for me—my lawyers, my agent—but the only person who didn't know what I wanted to do next was me. I'd been praying and agonizing over the new normal for months, and I still didn't really seem to have any clear guidance from God about any of it. My lawyers managed to get everything straightened with the district court and the school district, but I still didn't know what I would do the next fall.

As the holidays came around, I quit my job at the Tractor Supply Co. just to take some time off and really clear my head before the new year. I threw myself into home renovations and trying to reconnect with Jacob, who came to spend the month between Thanksgiving and Christmas with me and Denise after he was honorably discharged from the Marines. I still feel like I have a lot of time to make up for with him. I hope that we can get close again like we were when he was little, before I screwed all that up.

The weirdest thing is that I can see this was all a divine assignment, even though God sure had a sense of humor in picking me to be the poster boy for prayer. Looking back on my life, I see His fingerprints on every aspect of it—all the coincidences that so clearly were anything but. He took a genuinely bad kid who nobody wanted and did something remarkable and historic through me. It's crazy and humbling and weird all at the same time. I look back at my life and just have to laugh. My case will be a precedent studied in law schools for the next who knows how long—and yet, I will be the first to admit that there is nothing special about me.

I'm literally just an average Joe who God decided to use. I'm sure I wasn't His first choice. I probably wasn't even His hundredth choice. I guess I was just the one who, when I surrendered my life and told God I would do anything for Him, He decided to put that to the test.

Yet here I am, barely in my fifties with potentially half of my life left to live. I can't help but wonder what else God has planned for me. I think back to that ugly old tree at the boys' home that had weathered every storm, and part of me wants to find that next fight. Even though my case was a huge victory for freedom of religious expression and freedom of speech, these freedoms are by no means safe from attackers. They are under attacks both foreign and domestic every single day. We need people who will continually fight for our constitutional rights separate from religion, separate from politics—simply as American values. Whatever that next fight is, I'm down for it, and I sincerely hope future generations will rise to answer the call like a solitary sentry on a hill. Even though I'm no Bible scholar, I love the Scripture that says, "I have fought the good fight, I have finished the race, and I have remained faithful."[2] When I get to Heaven, I want God to tell me that I fought the good fight—even though it was difficult, even though it was costly.

There's something funny about looking back at my life and the fact that I was expelled from six schools, married three times, beaten up more times than I can count, almost blown up in Kuwait, stirring

---

2 2 Timothy 4:7 NLT

up actual crap in the burning fields in the Marines, and yet I have also met presidents and vice presidents, spoken in front of some of the most elite audiences in America, and landed in the legal history books—all for praying. I went from being an unwanted kid at a youth ranch to being invited back years later to lead a devotion with the boys. Ray, Dale, and Ms. Frederick were all still working there. Talk about coming full circle! Throughout the craziness I have seen in my life, the Marine Corps motto—Semper Fi—carries special meaning because I have seen that God has been "always faithful," even when I questioned.

While I may not know what's next in my personal journey, I know the One who does. I know in His time, He will reveal the next steps to me. In the meantime, I will continue to pray, I will continue to be ready to fight, and I will continue to wait on the Lord to renew my strength. I like the Scripture that says those who trust in the Lord, "will run and not grow weary. They will walk and not faint."[3]

Talk about coincidence. Looking back at my crazy life, it just goes to show that God can use any willing vessel, no matter how average that person may be.

---

3 Isaiah 40:31 NLT